Dedicated to Daniel Radack, my husband and soulmate.

Thanks to Elaine Cassell, Diana Lazarus, Susan Maguire and Natalie Adler who insisted that I write a book, and to Audrey Wolf who made me really believe that I could and attempted to sell it to major publishers. David Luban, Daniel Ellsberg and others tried to interest alternative publishers on my behalf. Thanks also to Marsha K.D. Foss for her support and careful copyediting, to Laura Gosse for her web expertise, and to Barbara Hoffman for her legal guidance with all things literary.

The actual publication of this book is nothing short of a miracle, which could not have been achieved without the editorial skills of Richard Bell, the sheer belief of Ray McGovern that this story needed to be out there, and the tireless work of Susan Krueger, whose effort is paralleled only by her heart and her convictions. And a special thank you to Jamie Krueger for her Jill-of-all-trades assistance. The beautiful cover would not be possible without Ben Baker's photography and without the assistance of Samantha Smith and Susan Krueger in creating the cover design.

I appreciate more than I can adequately put into words everyone who has stood beside me during my past five years in the wilderness.

The Canary in the Coalmine:
Blowing the Whistle in the Case of
"American Taliban" John Walker Lindh
A Memoir By Jesselyn Radack

This book is purely the opinion of the author. It is based on articles that can be found at www.patriotictruthteller.net. But it is a also book of memory, and memory has its own story to tell. I have done my best to be true to that story.

THE CANARY IN THE COALMINE:
BLOWING THE WHISTLE IN THE CASE OF "AMERICAN TALIBAN" JOHN WALKER LINDH

Advance praise for The Canary in the Coalmine:

This is a riveting – and chilling – account of how far the Bush Administration's Justice Department will go to destroy a critic.

ANTHONY LEWIS
New York Times

This book offers a poignant illustration of the erosion of civil rights and liberties in the "war on terrorism." It brings into sharp focus the critical question of whether we can respond effectively to the new threat of terrorism without jeopardizing the very freedoms and fundamental principles that characterize a democratic society.

NADINE STROSSEN
President, American Civil Liberties Union

**A memoir by
Jesselyn Radack
Copyright 2006**

The conscientious employee is often portrayed as vengeful, unstable, or out for attention. I have not been completely immune from these accusations, but the terms that have been used by what the press cites as "anonymous Justice Department officials" to describe me are far more incendiary: "traitor," "terrorist sympathizer," "turncoat," and "unpatriotic." Never mind that in debate circles, the lowest form of argumentation is name-calling. For an Administration attempting to quell opposition through a campaign of secrecy and silence, neither the Bush White House nor the Ashcroft Justice Department were short of words.

One of this Administration's favorite tactics is to paint any sort of dissent or criticism – whether it comes from whistleblowers, anti-war protesters, or advocates of the politically unpopular – as disloyal at best and unpatriotic at worst. With a Crusader's fervor, Ashcroft warned in stark terms that critics who "scare peace-loving people with phantoms of lost liberty only aid terrorists, for they erode our national unity and diminish our resolve." In a ham-handed way, he tried to portray the expression of civil liberties concerns as treasonous. Such ill-considered exhortations have a very real chilling effect on the exercise of basic freedom of speech.

Although my story is different in its details, it shares many of the same elements with the experiences of other whistleblowers: abuse of government power, lack of due process (or any process at all), secrecy and silence, political overkill, and base vengefulness. The Administration's vindictive response to its critics goes beyond questioning their truthfulness, competence and motives: it seeks to destroy them.

In most cases of whistleblowing, the Executive Branch attacks the person rather than the substance of his or her complaint. It shoots the messenger rather than addressing the message. It silences the critic rather than answering the criticism. It engages in intimidation, character assassination and professional destruction of those who break the code of silence. And it will not let go. As Jerome Doolittle, novelist and former White House speechwriter, characterized the Justice Department's venomous attacks on me: "There is something primordial about Team Bush's reaction to dissent, something reptilian. They're like the gila monster, its jaws holding their poisonous grip even after its head is severed."

"You are either with us or against us" – Bush's Procrustean mantra during his inexorable march to war in Iraq – applies with equal or greater force to those who cross him, and more broadly, to anyone he perceives as an "enemy." Ashcroft shares Bush's us-or-them mentality, and their categorical thinking is reflected in the increasingly deep division between "Red America" and "Blue America," a synecdoche that pollsters and political consultants use as shorthand for the U.S. population that is Republican and Democratic, respectively. Bush and Ashcroft also share a limitless capacity to nurse incandescent grudges. Ashcroft has made clear that forgiveness, while perfectly appropriate in religion, has no place at the Justice Department (except at his morning prayer meetings, of course). "The law is not about forgiveness," he said. "It is oftentimes about vengeance, oftentimes about revenge."

One of the most disturbing things about my story is that it's not an isolated incident. As bizarre, unbelievable and outrageous as it sounds, it is not uncommon. These vicissitudes have happened to everyone from military officers to Muslim guys playing paintball. It has even happened to other Justice Department attorneys.

I've decided to tell my story because I vowed that if I could ever speak safely again, I would not remain silent out of some sort of misplaced gratitude that I was no longer being threatened with termination, criminal prosecution, disbarment or ostracization.

My ordeal should have ended at many points along the trajectory. I was muzzled for over a year, so I have a lot of pent up things to say. Also, I feel a moral imperative to say them because if a person like me who enjoys relative privilege – being white, a U.S. citizen, educated, and comfortably middle-class – can so easily lose her freedom, then maybe people in this country can more easily understand the plight of those in post-9/11 America who are Arab or

Muslim, who are immigrants, who are poor, or who don't speak English.

A lot of commentators saw the John Walker Lindh case as an example of the government going after a minnow with a sledgehammer. The same thing can be said of my case writ small. This modus operandi has been dubbed "Ashcroft justice." Attorney General Ashcroft did not get the verdict he wanted against Lindh, in some measure, because of my actions. As CBS commentator Andrew Cohen noted in writing about my role,

> It was clear, although the government never explicitly conceded so, that prosecutors were open to a [plea bargain] deal with Lindh because of the brutal way in which he was treated by his military captors in Afghanistan and the spurious way in which federal law enforcement officials had observed Lindh's constitutional rights. It is no coincidence that the Lindh deal came about on the eve of a scheduled week-long [suppression] hearing that was going to bring into the open the specifics of how Lindh was treated and by whom.

In a classic case of "the lady doth protest too much," top officials at Justice took time out of their busy schedules to call Cohen after his article ran to try to convince him that he was wrong; specifically, that I had not caused the Lindh case to tank. They minimized me and downplayed my role in Lindh's surprise plea bargain.

If I really had nothing to do with the unraveling of the Lindh case (in the words of *The New Yorker*'s Jane Mayer, "the prosecution collapsed"), then query why Ashcroft and his functionaries are wasting so much time, energy and taxpayer money getting back at me. If I were a crank making wild allegations about the Lindh case, I would be ignored. But when the Assistant Attorney General starts throwing his weight around to keep me quiet, you have to wonder what I know.

Whether I played a large role or none at all, the government severely damaged my reputation and my psyche. It's hard to un-ring the bell. One person against an entire agency or government is a David versus Goliath struggle. In terms of raw power, the government holds all the cards. To sic the infinite resources of the American government on someone is more than a mismatched contest – it is tyranny. It is also a waste of, what we are reminded time and again are, precious and limited government resources.

It has been hard for me to write this memoir because I suffer from the cult of objectivity – the mistaken belief that impartiality will lend legitimacy to my story. But how can I be neutral when what I have experienced has been so personal and so driven by emotion, surmise, and partisan politics? I therefore confess up front that I have an ax to grind, and nearly $100,000 in legal bills to show for it.

I'm here to tell you that the emperor has no clothes, and that those who expose the nakedness of this Administration's policies and practices should be applauded, not annihilated. Public service does not mean blind obedience to one's supervisor or subservience to an agency agenda that subverts the law and the public interest. Deciding to blow the whistle can be the single most important decision an individual ever makes. It should not be a question of whether to blow the whistle, but of how loudly to blow it. And in doing so, public servants should not be forced to choose between their conscience and their career.

The past five years have been the most difficult of my life, but they have also been a cataclysmic growth period that has cemented my commitment to civil rights and liberties. I realize that there are many stories like mine, and that I am just a footnote in a seismic shift that is occurring in our country. But I promised myself that if I could ever speak freely again, then I would use my voice to try to prevent this sort of political revenge from happening to anyone else.

My saga began on September 11, 2001, as did the life-altering journeys of so many others.

2. Main Justice

I'm an attorney, though I am so disgusted by the behavior of some of the lawyers in my ordeal that I'm tempted to leave the profession and join the ranks of recovering lawyers who have seen the light. But then, I'd be giving John Ashcroft exactly what he wants: for me to quit the practice of law.

In 1995, I graduated from Yale Law School and joined the Department of Justice through the prestigious Attorney General's Honors Program, the recruitment mechanism for entry-level attorneys and the only way the Department hires graduating law students. Nearly 5,000 graduating law students from around the country applied for approximately 150 slots. A whopping third of my class applied to the Program. The Civil Division hired two of us in the Class of '95.

That same year, a politician named John Ashcroft became the junior senator from Missouri. A devout member of the Assemblies of God, a Pentecostal denomination that disapproves of drinking, pre-marital sex, cursing and dancing, Ashcroft routinely likened his political career to the life and death of Jesus Christ, referring to his campaign victories as "resurrections" and comparing his political defeats to "crucifixions." This was a resurrection. As described in his 1998 book, *Lessons From a Father to His Son*, his friends

10

anointed him with Crisco oil from the kitchen, marking his apotheosis in the style of "the ancient kings of Israel."

The Honors Program had long been viewed as a premiere opportunity for ambitious rookie lawyers – a plum assignment – and it was definitely my dream job. It offered excellent trial advocacy training, an opportunity to serve the public, and the chance to actually see the inside of a courtroom much sooner than if I had had to pay my dues behind the locked library doors of a law firm. More importantly, it guaranteed health and life insurance – coverage I could not obtain privately because I have MS, a serious "pre-existing medical condition," a daunting reality for a 24-year-old.

Little did I know that the Honors Program, founded by President Eisenhower's first attorney general and long overseen by career attorneys, would later be taken hostage by Ashcroft and his acolytes. When I started, the Honors Program was highly competitive, well-regarded, and had the laudable distinction of being apolitical. Ashcroft decided in 2002 that the Program would benefit from more direct participation by him and other political appointees. The Bush II Administration, which made clear its intention of stacking the federal bench with political conservatives, was aiming to do the same within the career ranks at Justice. Moreover, Ashcroft thought the Program had too many Ivy League graduates (apparently failing to realize that Ivy League schools comprised five of the top ten law schools in the country) and needed more candidates from the likes of his *alma mater.* I would have never made it under today's regime.

I joined the Department of Justice's Civil Division and practiced constitutional tort litigation for four years. In English, that means I defended the United States and individual federal officials against allegations of constitutional and statutory violations. In the so-called *Bivens* section, named for the Supreme Court case that authorized such lawsuits, we used to make fun of the *pro se* tax protestors, jailhouse lawyers, anti-government militias and other "frequent filers" who loved to sue the United States. Little did I know that someday I would be a plaintiff in such an action.

I was a true believer. The Department could not have found a more loyal, enthusiastic, flag-waving employee. I really believed that the government wore the white hat. I loved having the imprimatur of the United States behind me when I appeared in federal court. I liked feeling that I was always on the morally correct side of whatever the issue.

Litigation was a great way to cut my teeth as a new lawyer. However, the *Bivens* section, jokingly referred to by my future husband as the "vivisection" for its unforgiving hours and unstable directors, was incompatible with my life as it evolved beyond the office. The icing on the cake of my courtroom days was a federal jury trial in a godforsaken locale while I was seven months pregnant with our second son, Sam. I won the trial, but afterwards, all that the jurors wanted to know was whether I was having a boy or a girl, when the baby was due, and whether or not my co-counsel (who had the same last name) was my brother or my husband (he was neither). I took it as a sign that it was time to leave litigation.

Luckily, during the preceding seven months I had been detailed part-time to the Justice Department's newly-created Professional Responsibility Advisory Office (PRAO), pronounced "pray-oh," which rendered ethics advice to Department attorneys nationwide. The office was established in the aftermath of the McDade Amendment, an onerous little law that subjected Department of Justice attorneys not only to their own state bar rules, but also to the bar rules of any state in which they litigated. This statute created vertical and horizontal conflicts of law because most Department attorneys have a multi-jurisdictional practice.

I found legal ethics fascinating, challenging and important, and being a legal advisor offered me an opportunity to leave behind the travel, deadlines and general acrimony of litigation. Moreover, it was rare and exciting in a calcified bureaucracy like the Department of Justice to be a part of a fledgling office in its infancy, rather than one that was so entrenched and established, as most were.

After my maternity leave, I started as a full-time legal advisor at PRAO on Valentine's Day of 2000. There are three layers of security for Department attorneys – "confidential," "secret," and "top secret" – and this position required "top secret" clearance. I soon underwent my five-year "background re-investigation," which I passed with flying colors.

13

I had always tried to be ethically meticulous while working for the Department of Justice. I remembered vividly that during law school, Zoe Baird, the wife of one of my professors, had lost her chance to be the first female Attorney General because she neglected to pay taxes for her household help. I was fastidious about properly paying our "nanny taxes," even though I knew of many Justice colleagues, attorneys no less, who did not. Now that I was working at PRAO, the "ethics office," I felt that it was even more incumbent upon me to do things by the book.

PRAO was housed in the National Theatre Building – tony office space by government standards. At lunch I could go skating at Pershing Park Ice Rink across the street, an added bonus for a former figure skater. I loved my new job and seemed to have a knack for legal ethics.

The newly-hired director, Claudia Flynn, was a very astute and together-looking woman. Her elegant stature, fiery red hair, flawless makeup, and immaculate dress made her striking. We had gone to the same college, so we shared a bond. I really looked up to her.

Much to my delight, in September Claudia gave me a $2000 cash performance award, signaling that I had excelled during my first seven months as a permanent attorney at PRAO. With Claudia's backing, I started writing a law review article on the negative effects of the McDade Amendment, the legislation that was the impetus for our office. The article was accepted for publication by *The Georgetown*

Journal of Legal Ethics, the nation's premier legal ethics periodical and the only law journal to which PRAO subscribed.

In January 2001, Larry Thompson, a former U.S. Attorney then in private practice in Atlanta, published an article in *The Federal Lawyer* on how the McDade law was *good* for the profession – a position 180 degrees opposite from the one I had taken in my article. In February, it became public that President Bush intended to appoint Thompson, an African-American, to the high-profile post of Deputy Attorney General, a move designed in part to deflect criticism that Attorney General Ashcroft, chosen by President Bush to win points with social conservatives, was insensitive to race. (For example, Ashcroft had given the 1999 commencement address at Bob Jones University, a fundamentalist and racist institution. As a senator, he had also denied the first black Missouri Supreme Court Justice, Ronnie White, a federal judgeship for being "pro-criminal," when Ashcroft's real grudge was that White had outsmarted him by defeating a draconian pro-life measure.)

A draft of my law review article was in Thompson's briefing book, which was provided to him to prepare for his confirmation hearing. In March, I sent him the latest version of the article because I knew it took a position on the McDade Amendment – that the law had hampered federal prosecutors in carrying out their duties – that was diametrically opposed to his. I also knew that three senators on the Judiciary Committee had introduced proposals

15

to amend the McDade Amendment and that Thompson would be quizzed about it.

Before his hearing, Thompson called me at home to discuss the McDade law. He had not realized it was having such unintended consequences for Department attorneys. We became e-mail buddies of sorts during the unsettling months leading up to his confirmation. I think he was just venting from the stress of it all and I was a sympathetic ear. Sure enough, during the confirmation hearing he was grilled by Senator Patrick J. Leahy, ranking Democrat on the Judiciary Committee, about the McDade Amendment and was able to deftly respond that he had only recently learned of the problems it was causing for Justice attorneys. In early May, he was confirmed and sworn-in.

He invited me to lunch in June. One of his Associate Deputy Attorneys General told me it was a huge deal to make it onto Thompson's schedule, and that I was just before Paul O'Neill, the Secretary of Treasury. The Associate Deputy also recommended that I be open with Claudia about how cozy I was getting with Larry (we were on a first-name basis by then), especially since it could lead to a job change for me.

I told Claudia about my budding friendship with Larry and my upcoming lunch with him. I also told her that I would be interested in doing a detail to his office, or seeking a political appointment. She seemed surprised, but supportive.

On June 14, 2001, Larry and I shared a delightful lunch in his new office and discussed the possibility of my serving as Counsel for him.

People often ask me if I felt a big shift from a Reno Justice Department to one run by Ashcroft. The answer is, not at first. It is true that Ashcroft liked a corporate "top-down" model and valued secrecy, which stood in stark contrast to Reno's general policy of *glasnost* and reputation for endless briefings. However, Ashcroft's style was in keeping with Bush's strict code of loyalty and Rumsfeld's "command climate." Also, a chilly relationship developed between Ashcroft's people and career Justice attorneys. The Ashcroft hires regarded the career attorneys with suspicion, accused them of being too liberal, and effectively cut the career folks out of many policymaking decisions.

But for the most part, Ashcroft, humbled by the humiliating loss of his Senate seat (he lost to Missouri Governor Mel Carnahan, who had died *before* the election) and a bruising confirmation fight (he had received 42 negative votes, the most ever cast against a nominee for Attorney General), seemed content to lay low, host early-morning prayer gatherings on government property, and quietly serve as the Bush Administration's symbolic ambassador to the right.

For me, the sea change was not so much the change in Administration, but rather September 11, 2001, which changed the lives of everyone in our country and created a virtual revolution inside the Justice Department. On that fateful morning, Ashcroft and four aides were on a government plane en route to Milwaukee when a call came in on Ashcroft's secure phone line. He hung up and announced, "Our world has changed forever."

John Ashcroft changed too. Before September 11th, he couldn't have cared less about terrorism. Four months before the diabolical attacks, he didn't even mention terrorism in a memo outlining priorities for the Justice Department. But September 11th reinvigorated him and opened the door to his commitment to "creative destruction." He went from being embattled and disengaged to being a man on a mission. The detached and sedate Ashcroft was replaced by a defiant, pugnacious and polarizing zealot who dove into the war on terrorism with an enthusiasm that made his fierce opposition to abortion and gun control look like Victorian high tea. His draping of the female "Spirit of Justice" statue was not just a puritanical act; it was a metaphorical one.

3. 9/11 and the Fall

I remember Claudia's grabbing me from my office on her way upstairs to watch the conference room TV – a plane had just flown into the World Trade Center. On the screen was a live broadcast of smoke streaming from one of the towers in the aftermath of an obviously large explosion. The sky was clear and cerulean. The handful of us who had gathered all thought it was a freak mishap. As we watched the story unfold in real-time, a twin-engine Boeing going 400 miles an hour slammed into the other tower, exiting in a shower of flame and debris. In a collective gasp, all doubt was removed that this was no accident.

We all took turns calling our significant others on the conference room phone. No one wanted to stray from the TV. I called Dan. He was still at home with the children and completely unaware of what had happened.

"Dan, turn on the TV. Two planes just flew into the World Trade Center! They think it's terrorism. Don't take Jacob to nursery school yet."

Barbara Olson, a passenger on American Airlines Flight 77, phoned her husband, Solicitor General Theodore Olson, in the Justice Department. She told him that the plane had been hijacked. Twenty minutes later, the glass of sprawling windows facing Pennsylvania Avenue rattled and a dull boom shook the room

– the percussive effect of a 757 out of Dulles slamming into the Pentagon. We watched out the panoramic windows as people started streaming into the street below. Within minutes, a plume of rufous smoke silhouetted the Washington Monument.

Claudia said that we could leave. But it was unclear if we would be any safer in the chaos outside the building than in its comparatively safe confines. The FAA had shut down the air traffic system across the country, but the news reported that some planes were still in the air. At least inside we had access to phones, computers, radios, a TV and food. Moreover, getting home sounded like a logistical nightmare. The news reported that the Metro was not running and the bridges leaving D.C. were closed.

Just then, the south tower of the World Trade Center pancaked into the street, creating a massive noxious cloud of powder, debris and smoke. We watched open-mouthed.

Down the street, Secret Service agents armed with automatic weapons deployed into Lafayette Park across from the White House. The TV reported a car bomb at the State Department. We heard a tremendous explosion.

"Something just got hit," I said.

I later learned that the explosion was really a sonic boom emanating from F-16 fighter jets that had been scrambled from Langley Air Force Base in Hampton, Virginia, about 110 miles from the Pentagon. Trying to get to D.C. before any of the stray airplanes attacked, they hit Mach 2 – twice the speed of sound, about

20

1500 miles per hour – leaving a rolling acrosonic thunder all the way up Virginia.

A portion of the Pentagon collapsed. A fourth airliner, also hijacked, crashed near Pittsburgh. All of this occurred before 10:22 a.m., when the Justice Department was officially evacuated.

A few men in green military uniforms were shouting from bullhorns to evacuate. I grabbed a handful of chocolate mints and some bottles of water and stuffed them in my knapsack. I ducked back in the conference room one last time to check the news. I watched as the World Trade Center's north tower melted as if in slow motion, creating another tidal wave of dust and debris.

"I'm gone," I said to no one in particular.

On the way home, a state of emergency was declared in D.C. When I got home, I grasped Dan and the kids and broke down in sobs. I knew I had lost people I cared for and just didn't know about yet. The attack left nearly 3,000 dead.

After a night of bad dreams about trying to get home, I went back to work the next day for the sake of pretending everything was "business as usual" in the nation's capital. Nothing could have been further from the truth. I started trying to track people down. I stopped after speaking to the crying brother of an old friend, one of over 5000 now missing in New York. Brown University sent an e-mail to all alumni, asking people to reply if they or other alums they knew were safe. I replied on behalf of myself and Claudia. Military police in green camouflage stood sentry on street corners. Sirens and helicopters blared throughout the day. We were evacuated twice for bomb scares.

To the extent that Department attorneys had been risk-averse about the ethical propriety of their conduct – perhaps a bit too much so after the passage of the McDade Amendment – after September 11th it was quite the opposite. People had no fear. Anything and everything could and would be done in the name of fighting terrorism.

It reminded me of journalist Tom Friedman's description of "Hama Rules" in *Beirut to Jerusalem,* and how Hama Rules are no rules at all. The triumvirate of Bush, Ashcroft and Rumsfeld created their own version of Hama Rules, crushing people and leveling cities to uproot terrorists and eradicate the problem of Muslim extremists. There was a toxic and intoxicating miasma of moral superiority, machismo, self-righteousness and revenge. Bush's approach also perpetuated a belief that our government couldn't keep us secure within the current confines of due process, respect for freedoms of speech and association, and the normal system of checks and balances. In the words of President Bush, "Our nation recognizes that this new paradigm – ushered in not by us, but by terrorists – requires new thinking in the law of war."

I'm still searching, with both the benefit and burden of hindsight, for what caused the breakdown in PRAO and the Justice Department more generally. Certainly, government employees from the top-down were affected by the events of September 11th in a very personal way. Solicitor General Ted Olson's wife, Barbara, was killed aboard the plane that crashed into the Pentagon. A total of 125 people in the Pentagon died – 22 soldiers, 47 Army civilian employees, six Army contractors, 33 sailors, six Navy civilian employees, three Navy contractors and eight other Defense Department employees.

Rosh Hashanah, the Jewish new year, came one week later. The liturgy, which I had read faithfully for decades, was imbued with new meaning.

The opening blessing over the candles could not have been more appropriate: "Grant us this year a glimpse of the light of redemption, the light of healing and of peace."

The rabbi chanted with urgent emphasis in his voice, "Blessed is God for giving us life, for sustaining us, and for enabling us to reach this season." His words gave me the chills. A friend of mine had not reached the new season. I just didn't know it yet.

The rabbi intoned: "Grant us peace, your most precious gift. . . Bless our country, that it may always be a stronghold of peace, and its advocate among the nations." I pondered those words as our nation embarked on a long-term campaign against terrorism and a short-term attack on the al Qaeda terrorist network and its leader, Osama bin Laden. "Let peace descend on us . . . and all the world."

Would we let it?

On September 25th, John Yoo, a contemporary of mine from law school who now worked at the Justice Department's powerful Office of Legal Counsel, drafted a secret memo that landed on the desk of White House Counsel Alberto Gonzales. It said there were effectively "no limits" on Bush's powers to respond to the attacks of September 11th, and that the President's decisions "are for him alone and are unreviewable."

Black September came to a close. Wall Street ended its worst week in 68 years. I got a $3000 raise, which could not have been better timed given the troubled economy, and provided reassurance that I was performing well at work. I was grateful to be able to concentrate for more than two minutes. It was such a breakthrough when I could focus for two hours straight.

Jacob, my three-year-old, pegged me with impossible questions: Why did the bad guys make such a mess? Did they catch all of them? Are the bad guys going to do this again? I wanted so badly to say no, but could not. Jacob and his nursery school buddies were constructing Lego towers and knocking them over with plastic airplanes – acting out the unavoidable images that dominated TV and newspapers.

"Stop it," I said. "Please don't do that."

"It's just pretend, Mommy," Jake protested.

"But it's not," I said, realizing the futility of my argument.

When I read him "The Three Little Pigs," that night, he said he was glad our house was made of brick so that the Big Bad Wolf couldn't blow it down. How do you explain terrorism to a child?

At the end of September, D.C. was slammed by the most destructive tornado to hit the region in 75 years. Two University of Maryland students, sisters, were killed. I was disgusted with myself for deriving any joy or relief from the fact that it was a natural disaster that caused the ruin, not a man-made one.

During the first week in October, the Federal Reserve cut interest rates another half-point. It was the ninth cut that year as our country appeared to be sliding into a recession. We had to fly out of town because my mother was getting remarried. My family was originally routed out of Ronald Reagan Washington National Airport, but it was still closed, so we instead flew from Dulles, which had been used as a launching pad for the terrorist attacks less than a month earlier. For me and the majority of the other passengers, it was our first time flying since September 11th.

On the return flight, we were flying from the largest airport terminal in the world (Hartsfield Atlanta International Airport) into one of the nation's largest transatlantic gateways (Washington Dulles). The U.S. commenced air strikes against Afghanistan a couple of hours earlier, and the news was warning that retaliation was certain and imminent.

Instead of landing, we barely grazed the runway and angled up abruptly like a rocket. Confused looks came over all faces. At that strange moment, every passenger had the same thought: we've been hijacked. The cabin was

25

silent. No one was talking. No one was screaming. No one was crying. No one was reaching for his or her cell phone. Everyone was waiting. It was the longest two minutes of my life.

Finally, a terse voice emanated over the loudspeaker and explained that we had been forced to do a "touch-and-go" to avoid a Northwest Airlines plane in the runway. A touch-and-go is a procedure developed by the military to enable cadets to squeeze a few more takeoffs and landings into a training session. A hundred passengers sighed with relief. While later waiting in the aisle to exit, we talked about how we were afraid our plane had been turned into a guided missile. On the bus ride back to the terminal, we complained about how long it had taken for the captain to tell us what had really happened. While standing around the baggage carousel, we criticized the air traffic controllers, the airport, our airline, and the other airline.

I was so relieved that we had not been hijacked, that it was not until the next day, when a Scandinavian airliner hit a private jet on a runway in Italy killing all aboard, that I realized the magnitude of what had in fact happened to us. We were so busy being grateful for not getting hijacked, that no one bothered to thank the pilot for his quick-thinking and expert reflexes that saved us from a deadly collision. It was symptomatic of the aftermath of September 11th: we were so blinded by fear, we could not see the forest through the trees.

Castro. Gaddafi. Sadaam. Bin Laden had joined a rogue's gallery of the world's most notorious anti-American megalomaniacs. His videos spouting propaganda kept surfacing on Al-Jazeera, the Arab TV network. On the one-month anniversary of the attacks, the President gave a prime-time press conference. In a stark warning, the FBI said it had received information that there might be additional terrorist attacks domestically or abroad in the next several days.

Just when I thought the stress could get no worse, an anthrax bioterrorist attack began. Anthrax-laced letters created a baffling series of poisonings that touched the realm of postal workers, politicians, the news media, and those who were only incidentally exposed through cross-contamination from tainted mail. No one was safe. It started in Florida, where one employee lay dead and seven more exposed; New York had two people similarly affected; and there was a letter in Nevada containing powder, which tested positive for anthrax.

Then more anthrax letters surfaced, this time in D.C. Senate Majority Leader Thomas Daschle received one, and the Capitol closed as over 30 people tested positive for anthrax exposure. Two D.C. postal workers died of pulmonary anthrax and two more became seriously ill with this deadly inhaled form. It was unclear if this bioattack was bin Laden's handiwork or the doings of some unrelated homegrown menace. Everyone in D.C. was jittery. U.S. warplanes were still patrolling over our house throughout the night. The reign of terror had made us scared of our own shadow.

On October 26, 2001, the Department of Justice temporarily closed its mail facility in Landover, Maryland. The mail processed at the Landover facility comes directly from the Brentwood facility in D.C., where the two postal employees had died of pulmonary anthrax. That same morning, President Bush signed the awkwardly-titled "Uniting and Strengthening America by Providing Appropriate Tools Required to Intercept and Obstruct Terrorism Act of 2001," better known as the USA Patriot Act. It seemed as if Ashcroft started with the acronym, and then offered free tickets to his prayer sessions to whomever could come up with a name to fit it.

The Justice Department's Office of Legal Counsel – which was populated with Ashcroft's neocon policy wonks like John Yoo – worked with the White House Counsel's Office to hastily draft the sweeping anti-terrorism legislation. It called for far-reaching changes in federal law enforcement; for example, without a warrant and without probable cause, it gave the FBI new authority to search homes and offices and to monitor phone conversations and e-mail. It also gave federal investigators greater access to business, bank, credit, medical, and library records, and it affirmed the government's right to detain non-citizens without charges. The Patriot Act – expanding on the Antiterrorism and Effective Death Penalty Act of 1996, which itself was no friend to civil liberties – was rushed through Congress with lightning speed and virtually no debate.

A few days later, the Landover facility that processed mail for the Justice Department tested positive for anthrax bacteria. A New Jersey postal worker was found to have pulmonary anthrax, the thirteenth confirmed case since the outbreak began, including five in the D.C. region. Then we got another terror alert.

Ashcroft appeared before the TV cameras at all hours, usually wearing too much makeup and often with FBI Director Robert S. Mueller, III, soberly at his side, offering updates or bleak doomsday warnings. At the end of October, Mueller wrote me a letter thanking me for my article on the McDade Amendment. Frankly, I was surprised he had had the time to read it, given the obsessive focus on terrorism.

As if it wasn't enough to be worried about anthrax at work, environmental tests found traces of anthrax at our neighborhood post office. This was hitting too close to home, literally. On Halloween, a New York City hospital worker became the fourth person to die from pulmonary anthrax, which matched the anthrax involved in the other attacks. It was hard to get in the mood for ghosts and goblins. Things were scary enough already. It's only fun when it's make believe, but the fear was all too real.

November was no better. Osama bin Laden issued another video. We now had warnings of possible terrorist attacks on California bridges. President Bush had an 86%

approval rating. Ashcroft's was near 70%. Fear was a powerful force.

Major General Geoffrey D. Miller, who was to become a prominent figure in the spread of aggressive interrogation techniques to Iraq, took over the intelligence-gathering effort at Guantánamo Bay. Military police and intelligence units that had formerly been rivals were merged into a single task force. Interrogators, translators and analysts were divided into "tiger teams" to interview detainees. Guards were encouraged to single out the leaders among the prison population so that they could be isolated and marked for interrogation. By 2005, of more than 700 prisoners who passed through Guantánamo, only 12 were designated for trial by military commission. Of this meager number, only four have been charged. None has been tried or convicted.

Sometimes people engage in self-destructive behavior as a response to overwhelming tragedy. My armchair analysis is that our country is suffering from a collective post-traumatic stress disorder (PTSD) that permeates the highest levels of government and trickles down to the line employees. It is normal to develop adverse symptoms following an extremely stressful event such as a terrorist attack. Exposure to a situation that involves the threat of death or its imagined imminence can also trigger PTSD. Merely witnessing or observing death may also trigger adverse symptoms, which can include isolating oneself, hyper-vigilance, and severe anxiety. I don't know if some form of PTSD is what accounts for the political and legal excesses in the aftermath of September 11th. But I do know that none of us were behaving rationally. By accident of chance, I became involved in a pivotal event that exemplified this new hysteria.

4. The "American Taliban"

John Walker, eventually identified by his full name, John Walker Lindh, converted to Islam when he was sixteen-years-old. He embarked on a journey to Yemen in 2000 to study classical Arabic and Islamic theology. By the spring of 2001, however, he became convinced that it was incumbent upon devout Muslims to do more than just read and pray. He felt called to train for military *jihad*. In June 2001, he crossed the border into Afghanistan to volunteer for the Afghan army, which was engaged in a protracted civil war between the now-deposed Taliban government and the Northern Alliance.

Lindh viewed the Taliban, the *de facto* government of Afghanistan, as upholders of Islam. United States aid to the Taliban dated back to the Soviet invasion of Afghanistan, when the Taliban served as anticommunist opposition. During the Carter administration, the Reagan administration, the first Bush administration, the Clinton administration, and the second Bush administration, the United States provided the Taliban army with military and humanitarian assistance. The Russian government continued to fund the Northern Alliance up until 2001, the year Lindh joined the Afghan resistance movement. In his own words, Lindh "saw the war between the Taliban and the

Northern Alliance as a continuation of the war between the *mujahideen* and the Soviets," and wanted to be one of the freedom fighters.

In Lindh's naïve view, he was just helping to alleviate the suffering of oppressed Muslims against whom the Northern Alliance warlords were committing unspeakable atrocities. He wanted to be a soldier for the Islamic liberation movement against the warlords who controlled northern Afghanistan provinces and were subjugating ordinary citizens. In joining an Islamic paramilitary program run by a Pakistani organization that trained Muslims to fight against Indian security forces, he did not have a sophisticated understanding of the complex conflict between Pakistan and India over the disputed territory of Kashmir. Nor did he know that the Taliban had an atrocious human rights record.

Because of his language deficiencies, the Taliban recruiters made Lindh join al Ansar, a non-Afghan unit. He checked into an al Ansar training camp called al Farooq, where there were two kinds of courses: al Qaeda training to fight civilians, and military training to fight the Northern Alliance. Lindh did only the latter training, spending nearly eighteen hours a day praying, exercising, eating, learning about weapons and warfare, and performing routine chores.

A week before September 11th, he finally arrived on the Taliban's front line, where he performed sentry duty, which entailed a lot of down-time for quiet reading. After September 11th, he grew alienated from his comrades, but stayed on for fear of appearing to be a spy. Little did he know that his home country would soon view him as the traitor incarnate.

The United States began bombing Afghan targets in October, and started hitting Lindh's outpost by November 5th. By November 10th, his unit was in a panicked retreat to Kunduz. They fled fifty miles on foot over unforgiving desert terrain. Over a treacherous two days, they lost a third of their men. On November 21st, the regional Taliban military leader negotiated a surrender of the unit with the notoriously savage General Dostum of the Northern Alliance, who was a former Soviet collaborator-turned-warlord. Lindh's commander had agreed to pay Dostum in exchange for safe passage across Northern Alliance territory to the Taliban stronghold of Herat. From there, Lindh planned to escape to Pakistan and return home.

But Lindh's commander was double-crossed. The cash was paid, but the Northern Alliance took the Taliban soldiers prisoner and detained them at the ancient Qala-i-Jhangi fortress on the outskirts of Mazar-i-Sharif in northern Afghanistan. Qala-i-Jhangi was the military headquarters of Dostum. When a Taliban prisoner resisted, Northern Alliance guards herded the 400 prisoners into the basement of a sturdy, Soviet-built schoolhouse. Dostum's men dropped a grenade down an air duct, which narrowly missed Lindh but wounded or killed several of his fellow captives.

As memorialized in video footage, on November 25th, the prisoners were led out of the basement into the courtyard of the old fortress, made to kneel in rows, and kicked and beaten with sticks. Lindh was knocked in the head and nearly lost consciousness. The Northern Alliance and two armed CIA officers, Johnny "Mike" Spann and Dave Tyson, circulated among the prisoners.

Lindh was singled out and removed from the group for questioning. Without identifying himself and Tyson as agents of the U.S. government, Spann used an interrogation tactic of threatening Lindh with death.

"You believe in what you're doing here that much, you're willing to be killed here?" Spann asked in a video that was seen by millions in the days following Lindh's capture.

"He's got to decide if he wants to live or die, and die here," Tyson told Spann, within earshot of Lindh. "We're just going to leave him, and he's going to fucking sit in prison the rest of his fucking short life. It's his decision."

Lindh did not respond and was returned to the larger group of prisoners.

Suddenly an explosion and shouting marked a spontaneous uprising. The Northern Alliance troops reacted by shooting scores of bound, unarmed prisoners, many of whom died with their arms still tied behind their backs. The grisly revolt, in which Lindh was not a participant, led to Lindh's getting shot in the right thigh by an AK-47 bullet and to Spann's death – the first American to die in combat in the American-Afghan war.

Though neither man's injury was caused by the other, Lindh would later be charged with conspiracy to commit murder in the death of

Mike Spann. Even though the judge eventually found that "[t]he government has no evidence of that," the government would still bring Spann's parents and widow to the courthouse and stage an emotional press conference in which the Spann family denounced Lindh as a traitor and demanded that he be given the death penalty.

Lindh played dead for a day before Taliban soldiers helped him and other wounded survivors into the basement of a building in the fortress, where they would spend the next six harrowing days. The Northern Alliance tried to flush out the unarmed, wounded, starving prisoners who were holed up in the basement with gunfire, hand grenades, and ignited diesel fuel. Finally, the Alliance flooded the basement with freezing water, which quickly became polluted with blood, human waste and floating body parts.

Miraculously, Lindh and eighty-five others survived, and he was taken into military custody on December 1st. According to a secret document I obtained in June 2004, an Army intelligence officer "advised that before interviewing Lindh, instructions came from higher headquarters for him to coordinate with JSOTF [the Joint Special Operations Task Force] JAG officer. He was told . . . he could collect on anything criminal that was volunteered."

But Higher Headquarters told the intelligence officer more than that. Rumsfeld's office told him not to handle Lindh with kid gloves. In a stunning revelation, the document states: "The Admiral told him that the Secretary of Defense's counsel had authorized him to 'take

36

the gloves off' and ask whatever he wanted."
These instructions to get tough with Lindh,
contained in the document I have, are the
earliest known evidence that the Bush
Administration was willing to push the envelope
on how far it could go to extract information
from suspected terrorists.

In a reversal of the usual legal procedure,
according to this document, the "JAG had said
that if Lindh said anything incriminating, read
him his rights." Needless to say, it defeats the
purpose of Mirandizing someone to do so only
after they have already made incriminating
statements. The purpose of the Miranda
warning is to neutralize the distinct
psychological disadvantage that suspects are
under when dealing with interrogators. After a
person has been taken officially into custody,
but *before* any interrogation takes place, the
subject must be informed of his Miranda rights.
The Army intelligence officer "told the JAG he
did not have a copy of Miranda and asked
JSOTF to send Miranda by fax but he never got
it. He never gave Lindh the Miranda warnings."

U.S. Special Forces interrogated Lindh and
tied his hands with rope, pulled a hood over his
head, drove him for several hours, placed him in
a dark room, and taunted him with vulgar
epithets. Lindh repeatedly requested counsel,
but met with indifference.

Newsweek first broke the story, sensationally
dubbing Lindh the "American Taliban." That
night, Lindh's mother, Marilyn Walker, found an
MSNBC (a co-branded *Newsweek* site) article
describing a young American who had been

37

found among a group of Taliban prisoners of war in northern Afghanistan. He said he was twenty-years-old, had been born in Washington, D.C., was an American citizen and had converted to Islam. She called her ex-husband, Frank Lindh.

By the next morning, Marilyn Walker had spoken with the State Department, the ACLU, Amnesty International, and Human Rights Watch, and all had flatly declined to provide assistance. As Frank Lindh later explained:

> This was an especially painful moment for us. It appeared that John's case was so controversial, his cause so hopeless, that nobody would be willing to come to his defense. John was wounded and had nearly been killed under incredible circumstances on the other side of the world. As his parents, we felt desperate for help.

He then called legendary trial lawyer James Brosnahan, who agreed to meet him the next morning, December 3rd.

The public attention created nothing short of mass hysteria. By the time Jim Brosnahan and Frank Lindh met, virtually every American newspaper was running front-page stories about the "American Taliban," he was being discussed on every radio show, and images of him were constantly shown on TV. President Bush, Vice President Dick Cheney, Rumsfeld, Powell, Ashcroft, and Senators Hillary Clinton and John

McCain made inflammatory comments and prejudicial statements, none of them true, that Lindh was an al Qaeda fighter, terrorist and traitor; fired his weapon; attended a terrorist training camp; supported bin Laden; and had foreknowledge of September 11th – even though the government from the first day of Lindh's capture was in possession of facts to the contrary.

Lindh's parents tried to write to him through the International Red Cross, but were informed that the U.S. military authorities would not allow their letters through. The military authorities also refused the Red Cross's request to visit Lindh to check on his condition. Lindh would become the first American to be prosecuted as part of the Bush Administration's war on terrorism.

5. The Call

Shortly after meeting with Frank Lindh, Brosnahan faxed a letter to a number of key government officials, including Secretary of State Powell, Attorney General Ashcroft, Secretary of Defense Rumsfeld, CIA Director George Tenet, and CIA General Counsel Robert McNamara, Jr. The letter informed them that Brosnahan had been hired by Lindh's parents to represent their son and asked that any further interrogation of him be stopped.

On December 7th, Lindh was flown to Camp Rhino, a U.S. Marine base in the high Afghan desert south of Kandahar, a former stronghold of the Taliban regime. He was blindfolded, stripped naked, bound to a stretcher with duct tape, taunted, threatened and locked in an unheated metal shipping container that sat on the floor in the bitter cold. That day, on what I thought would be a laid-back Friday, I received a call from John De Pue, a counter-terrorism prosecutor in the Criminal Division's Terrorism and Violent Crime Section.

"The FBI wants to interview American Taliban member John Walker sometime next week," De Pue advised. "The interview would occur in Afghanistan. Walker's father retained counsel for him and the FBI wants to question Walker about taking up arms against the U.S."

This type of situation raised red flags at PRAO because the ethics rules prohibit communication with people represented by counsel. We were told unambiguously that Lindh had counsel. In the advice we later rendered, the premise that Lindh had counsel was never questioned. We never suggested for a minute the argument that he was somehow not "really" represented – the argument Ashcroft ultimately adopted.

I consulted with Claudia and a senior legal advisor, Joan Goldfrank. Our office, as was the case with many other offices at Justice, had been abuzz all week with news of the "American Taliban." The American people, still reeling from September 11th, were clearly out for blood. It was going to be the modern-day equivalent of a legal lynching, a term used for southern "show trials" of black men in death penalty cases. But this time the lynching would make an example of a Muslim man in a terrorism case.

What jurisdiction would he be tried in? Virginia was the most conservative. Was there any way to charge him with treason? It was one of the only offenses punishable by death. Had he killed the CIA agent Johnny Micheal Spann, who had died in the uprising at Mazar-e-Sharif where Lindh was held? Spann had interrogated Lindh for about 30 minutes before the start of the uprising.

The Department of Justice and the public at large had it in for Lindh. The hue and cry was deafening.

I responded that interviewing Lindh would not be authorized by law under the ethics rules. The rule of professional responsibility that governs contact by a lawyer with a person represented by counsel is set forth in the

American Bar Association (ABA) Model Rule of Professional Conduct 4.2, the "anti-contact rule," which was the Achilles heel of prosecutors. It stated that "[i]n representing a client, a lawyer shall not communicate about the subject of the representation with a person the lawyer knows to be represented by another lawyer in the matter, unless that lawyer has the consent of the other lawyer or is authorized by law to do so." The rule expressly provides for ex parte communications (without the consent of the represented person's lawyer) that are "authorized by law."

The majority of Circuit Courts, including those in which Lindh could be indicted, had held that covert (undercover), pre-indictment, non-custodial contacts with represented persons during criminal investigations do not violate the anti-contact rule. For example, it would be okay for an undercover agent or confidential informant to contact a represented person who had not been arrested or formally charged. But Lindh's situation struck out on two of those three criteria. His interview would be overt and custodial, and therefore was not authorized by law.

However, my colleagues and I still tried to think of some creative ways that the FBI could interview the "American Taliban" and stay within ethical boundaries; for example, I suggested that since his parents were saying publicly that they thought their son was brainwashed, the FBI could ask Lindh if he really wanted an attorney of their choosing.

By the end of the day, U.S. officials released a list of six possible charges, including treason, murder and conspiracy, that Lindh could face. Most carried a possible death sentence upon conviction.

On December 9th at Camp Rhino, after two days in the steel shipping container, Lindh was taken out. FBI agent Christopher Reimann began extracting the confession from Lindh that became the basis for the eventual and ill-advised criminal case. Reimann read Lindh the Maranda warning, but admits that when noting the right to counsel, he ad-libbed, "Of course, there are no lawyers here." Lindh was not told that his parents had retained an attorney for him who was willing to fly to Afghanistan. Worried that he would be returned to the container, which in fact happened at the conclusion of the two-day interrogation, Lindh signed the waiver, which was improperly administered and clearly raised voluntariness issues.

On Monday De Pue called again with news from the Deputy Legal Advisor of the FBI: despite our advice not to question Lindh without counsel, an agent went and interviewed him over the weekend.

De Pue wanted to know what to do now.

I was surprised that our advice was disregarded, but not shocked because the FBI had a reputation among the Justice Department for being a bunch of cowboys who did their own thing. What really surprised me was that the Criminal Division was so quick to confess error

top legal adviser and the government's principal interpreter of treaties, Taft wrote a blunt letter to Yoo in the Justice Department on January 11, 2002. It dispensed with the usual bureaucratic niceties and excoriated Justice's legal advice to President Bush about detainees as "legally flawed and procedurally impossible," its reasoning as "incorrect and incomplete," and its arguments as "contrary to the official position of the United States, the United Nations and all other states that have considered the issue."

Less than a month after I closed the Lindh file, the Department of Justice filed criminal charges against him. Another surprise. With much fanfare, Attorney General Ashcroft, who had a reputation for being a showboat, announced the filing of criminal charges on January 15th. Although the government's own evidence showed that Lindh had done nothing more than volunteer as a foot soldier in the Afghan army, Ashcroft began his dramatic televised statement by referring to September 11th and saying, "We cannot overlook attacks on America when they come from United States citizens." He claimed that Lindh had "knowingly and purposely allied himself with certain terrorist organizations," and that he had "embraced" those who "had murdered thousands of his countrymen." The statement violated Justice Department guidelines on the release of information related to criminal proceedings, which are intended to ensure that a defendant is not prejudiced when such an announcement is made.

A reporter stood up. "Sir, even though he was Mirandized, his family has complained several times that they haven't had the chance to get his lawyer in to talk to him yet. Do you know how soon his lawyer will have access to him now that these charges have been filed?"

"Well, I think it's important to understand that the subject here is entitled to choose his own lawyer," the Attorney General explained, "and to our knowledge, has not chosen a lawyer at this time."

In an about-face from the operative facts with which I was provided – that Lindh was represented by counsel – Ashcroft appeared to be saying that the lawyer whom Lindh's father had hired to represent him was not legitimate because Lindh had not personally retained him. What Ashcroft neglected to mention was that the lawyer had sent letters to him, Rumsfeld, Powell, Tenet and McNamara informing them that he represented Lindh and wanted to meet with his client, and that those efforts were deliberately blocked. For more than fifty days after receiving Brosnahan's letter, the government continued to hold and interrogate Lindh without giving him access to legal counsel and without telling him his family had retained a lawyer to represent him.

The day after the overblown press conference, the first suspected al Qaeda and Taliban prisoners began arriving at the U.S. prison camp on Guantánamo Bay, Cuba, which presumably would have been John Walker Lindh's fate if he had not been a U.S. citizen.

Based on the advice of White House and Justice Department lawyers, on January 18th, President Bush initially decided that the Geneva Conventions would not apply to the conflicts with al Qaeda and the Taliban, and Rumsfeld sent a memo to that effect to the chairman of the Joint Chiefs of Staff.

Unbeknownst to me, on January 22nd, Claudia faxed three of my e-mails about Lindh to Ken Melson, the Criminal Chief of the U.S. Attorney's Office for the Eastern District of Virginia, which had jurisdiction over Lindh and the majority of other terrorism cases that the government would later bring. That same day, the Justice Department sent a 37-page memo, authored by Assistant Attorney General Bybee, to the White House and Pentagon, which argued that the War Crimes Act (a 1996 law that carries the death penalty) and the Geneva Conventions did not apply to al Qaeda prisoners and that President Bush had constitutional authority to "suspend our treaty obligations toward Afghanistan" because it was a "failed state."

Lindh arrived back in the United States on January 23rd, chained up in a military plane. He was helicoptered to the Alexandria city jail, where his parents tried to visit him but were turned away.

The next morning Lindh had his first court appearance, where he met his lawyers for the first time in a brief, 10-minute conference before the preliminary hearing. Judge T. S. Ellis, III, set a trial date for late August, thereby ensuring that Lindh would be on trial just a few miles from the Pentagon on the one-year anniversary of September 11th. The defense team was deeply troubled by the timing, especially in light of Ashcroft's intemperate remarks.

On January 25th, White House Counsel Alberto Gonzales wrote a memo to President Bush concluding that the Justice Department's advice in the January 9th memo was sound and that the President should declare the Taliban and al Qaeda outside the protections of the Geneva Conventions because the war on terrorism "renders obsolete Geneva's strict limitations on questioning of enemy prisoners and renders quaint some of its provisions."

The next day, Secretary of State Colin Powell wrote a memo to White House Counsel Gonzales, making clear that the advantages of applying the Geneva Conventions far outweighed their rejection. Powell's dissent argued that declaring the conventions inapplicable would "reverse over a century of U.S. policy and practice in supporting the Geneva Conventions and undermine the protections of the law of war for our troops, both in this specific conflict and in general." He also said, with great prescience, it would "undermine public support among critical allies."

The following day, Secretary Rumsfeld made his first visit to Guantánamo Bay and declared that the prisoners there "will not be determined to be POWs."

At our weekly staff meeting on January 29th, Claudia announced that our office had been taking a more conservative position lately. That was an understatement. That same day, President Bush said the detainees at

Guantánamo would not be treated as prisoners of war, though their exact legal status was still being "worked out."

On February 1, 2002, Ashcroft sent Bush a 12-paragraph memo warning in stark terms, as Ashcroft was inclined to do, that if the President sided with the State Department about the Geneva Conventions, American officials might wind up going to jail for violating U.S. and international laws. Ashcroft's memo should have raised red flags. It summarized the Justice Department's position on why the Geneva Conventions did not apply to al Qaeda and Taliban detainees and served as Ashcroft's personal one-fingered salute to the State Department.

Taft, on behalf of the State Department, wrote a memo the next day to White House Counsel Gonzales, reiterating Powell's warning that the broad rejection of the Geneva Conventions could put U.S. troops at risk. "A decision that the conventions do not apply to the conflict in Afghanistan in which our armed forces are engaged deprives our troops there of any claim to the protection of the Convention in the event they are captured." Furthermore, rcfusing Geneva standards to detainees "weakens protections afforded by the Conventions to our troops in future conflicts." The State Department memo also advised that following Geneva standards "demonstrates that the United States bases its conduct not just on its policy preferences, but on its international legal obligations."

An attachment to the memo noted that CIA lawyers asked for an explicit understanding that their operatives were exempt from the Administration's public pledge to abide by the spirit of the Geneva Conventions.

On February 4th, Claudia strode into my office as if she were on a mission, shut the door behind her, and handed me a performance evaluation.

It was not the usual time for evaluations. And it wasn't as if they were just being distributed to everybody late. No one else had received one. Curiously, it was unsigned. It also covered a nine-month rating period (the usual was three months) that had ended four months earlier.

"I know what's in here will come as a shock to you," she warned, "but you just don't seem happy working here. . ."

I conceded that I wasn't happy with Joan Goldfrank's pettiness and jealousy in the aftermath of my *Georgetown* article and amity with Larry Thompson, but that I loved legal ethics.

"Well, I think you need to find a new job. Otherwise, I'll have to put this evaluation in your permanent personnel file."

This seemed like an extreme edict, but I had not yet read the evaluation.

When I did so, it was beyond blistering. It was downright cruel. I started crying because no one had ever said such vicious things about me. Moreover, it was filled with blatant lies. For example, it said: "In one matter, she drafted a motion for an AUSA in which she failed to present a routine legal issue . . . in a correct, coherent fashion. . . . The draft by Ms. Radack was deficient in its organization, in the arguments it presented and in its rendition of the issues and the legal authorities." The AUSA with whom I had drafted the motion, David Cortes, had chosen to submit the motion we drafted together instead of the weak revision drafted by one of my supervisors. The motion was granted and the judge thought the matter important enough, because it carved new legal ground in North Carolina that was helpful to the government, to publish his opinion, which was based verbatim on the motion. The judge's opinion in *United States v. Joseph Binder Schweizer Emplem Co.* was later cited favorably in the ABA Annotated Model Rules of Professional Conduct, the legal ethics bible.

The classic line in the performance evaluation, and the one that was most telling, excoriated me for being, essentially, too uppity: "She took inappropriate actions that indicated that she did not understand her role in the office viz-a-viz higher level officials." In other words, by accepting Larry Thompson's lunch invitation, I had stepped out of my place.

This theme was repeated throughout the vituperative evaluation: "With respect to understanding her position in the office . . . Ms. Radack contacted a senior official in the office of the Deputy Attorney General without the knowledge or approval of anyone in PRAO, including the Director [Claudia Flynn] who reports directly to the official in question. These communications manifest a serious lapse in judgment by Ms. Radack." It appeared that my friendship with Larry had embarrassed Claudia.

The evaluation was so over the top – and contradicted by my professional track record (a merit bonus less than a year earlier, a groundbreaking published judicial opinion based on a brief I had written, a law review article in a prestigious journal, a raise, and recognition from senior agency heads) – that it was clear something else was going on. I just didn't yet know or understand what.

Claudia's threat that the vitriolic evaluation would be placed in my personnel file if I did not leave was something I took seriously because I planned on being a career civil servant and relied on my unblemished academic and employment record towards that end. Moreover, my government job was my only ticket to guaranteed health and life insurance as someone with multiple sclerosis.

The very next day, Ashcroft held a press conference and demagogically announced Lindh's formal indictment.

"John Walker Lindh chose to train with al Qaeda, chose to fight with the Taliban, chose to be led by Osama bin Laden," Ashcroft stated. "[T]he fact of those choices is clear. Americans who love their country do not dedicate themselves to killing Americans." Even William F. Buckley's conservative *National Review* criticized Ashcroft's prejudicial statements about a pending prosecution as "inappropriate" and "gratuitous."

In a bold and unflinching statement, Ashcroft claimed with a straight face, "At each step in this process, Walker Lindh's rights . . . have been carefully, scrupulously honored."

I knew Ashcroft was lying, but I still did not put two and two together.

6. The Cover-Up

On February 7, 2002, Bybee of the Justice Department advised White House Counsel Gonzales that the President had "reasonable factual grounds" to determine that Taliban fighters captured in Afghanistan were not entitled to prisoner of war status.

There was a seemingly irresolvable schism, with State Department officials and military lawyers on one side and the White House, Department of Justice and Defense Department on the other. Later that day, President Bush issued a directive that settled the scorched-earth memos battle in favor of the Department of Justice: the Geneva Conventions would apply to Taliban prisoners, but not to al Qaeda prisoners. Bush said that he believed he had "the authority under the Constitution" to deny protections of the Geneva Conventions to combatants picked up during the war in Afghanistan, but that he would "decline to exercise that authority at this time." In one of his infamous mixed messages, he simultaneously declared that all Taliban detainees were "unlawful combatants" who were not entitled to prisoner of war status. You figure it out.

The criminal case against Lindh continued to proceed at lightning speed in the Eastern District of Virginia, known nationally as the "rocket docket" for its precision-like disposition of important cases. On February 15th, U.S. District Court Judge T.S. Ellis, III, who was presiding over the Lindh case, issued a discovery order. In essence, it ordered that all copies of the Justice Department's internal correspondence about the conditions of Lindh's interrogation be sent to him so that he could determine if the documents should be passed on to the defense team. Claudia concealed the order from me.

A week later, again without telling me that she was circulating my e-mail to senior Department officials, Claudia faxed to Alice Fisher, the Deputy Assistant Attorney General of the Criminal Division, the same three e-mails she had faxed a month earlier to Ken Melson.

On February 26th, Bybee sent a memo from the Justice Department to the Pentagon's general counsel, Haynes, arguing that the constitutional protections against self-incrimination do not apply to detainees at Guantánamo Bay because they are not being tried in U.S. criminal courts.

In March 2002, the CIA established a secret prison in Thailand to house Abu Zabayda, the first important al Qaeda target captured. The public did not learn about the CIA's secret prisons until November 2005, when news broke that the CIA maintains its own network of secret prisons ("black sites") into which 100 or more terrorist suspects had "disappeared," as if victims of a Third World dictatorship. Two CIA secret prisons were operating in Eastern Europe until they were shut down following Human Rights Watch reports of their existence in Poland and Romania. Another CIA prison is in the North African desert.

March 7, 2002, was the pivotal day for me, when two and two finally added up to four. I got to work to find an e-mail from Assistant U.S. Attorney Randy Bellows, the lead prosecutor in the Lindh case. He informed me that he had filed with the court two of my e-mails with De Pue, but wanted confirmation that he had all Lindh-related communications I had written so that he could comply with the Court's discovery order. I wondered, What discovery order? His contact was my first alert to the discovery order. No one within PRAO had advised me of the Court's order or asked me to assist with compliance, even though I was the author and most likely source of the materials sought by the Court. Moreover, I had written far more than two e-mails.

Why was Bellows contacting me, a junior attorney, directly? Numerous people have suggested to me that Bellows was doing due diligence because he was keenly aware of Justice Department discovery violations from his work as the head of the Attorney General's Review Team, which submitted a 778-page internal report (commonly referred to as the "Bellows Report") in May of 2000 that was eventually made part of Congressional oversight hearings. It investigated the FBI's bungling of the Wen Ho Lee case and discussed, for example, how during the trial of Oklahoma City bomber Timothy McVeigh, the Justice Department and the FBI failed to turn over to the defense more than 4,400 pages of FBI documents on the case. This error forced Ashcroft to stay McVeigh's execution for a month.   Bellows didn't want to get similarly burned.

I was concerned immediately because I knew there were many more e-mails than the couple Bellows possessed.   I didn't think anything suspect was going on, just that there had been some kind of major bureaucratic error and that it needed to be corrected as soon as possible.   Claudia wasn't in yet, so I forwarded Bellows' e-mail to her and emphasized that there were more e-mails generated by our office than the two that he had.

Claudia came in shortly afterwards and I rushed to tell her in person about this development. She got very defensive. Staring daggers at me, she whispered in a slow, deliberate voice, "I sent *everything* that was in the file."

This was news to me.   It was the first I learned that my e-mails had been sent to anyone besides John De Pue, my original correspondent. I told Claudia that I knew of substantially more relevant e-mails than the two that Bellows possessed.

I went and checked the hard copy file, which had been an inch-thick stack of paper bound by a heavy-duty, long-reach staple. I felt sick as soon as I saw what was – and what was not – inside.   A fist-sized knot formed in my stomach. The file contained only three e-mails – very innocuous e-mails. The three that were in there did not even seem logical. There was our initial advice, but nothing from the we-ignored-your-advice-and-did-it-anyway aftermath. There was a reply from De Pue, but not the underlying message from me. And there was the final e-mail saying that Lindh had been Mirandized and therefore De Pue was closing the file on his end. I had submitted more than a dozen e-mails for the file, all of which I had personally stapled to the "Inquiry Data Sheet," which ensures that documents are properly filed.

I was alarmed because whatever had transpired seemed so deliberate. Claudia was the last person to have handled the file, as evidenced by the fax cover sheets. Her handwriting was literally all over the two fax cover sheets indicating that she sent the three surviving e-mails to Ken Melson and Alice Fisher. Claudia had never informed me that my e-mails had been sent to anyone besides John De Pue.

I immediately confided in Donald Mackay, a trusted and seasoned colleague on the verge of retirement, who had served six years as the U.S. Attorney for the Southern District of Illinois. He examined the file and said very matter-of-factly, "This file has been purged."

I had never heard that expression – "purged" – used in the context of a government file. The word made me think of bulimic adolescent girls, not top-ranked government officials. Besides, it was just inconceivable. At that time, the Department of Justice was pursuing accounting giant Arthur Anderson for obstruction of justice for destroying documents related to the Enron investigation. How was this different?

I was confronted with an unmistakable intimation to overlook violations of law. My new understanding imposed unpalatable choices between the threat of discipline for insubordination, potential liability for knowingly sanctioning violations of law, or violating government ethics rules by remaining a silent observer who passively acquiesces to betrayals of the public trust.

"What should I do?" I asked Don.

"You need to cover your ass, that's what," he said. "Call the computer help line, retrieve as many of those e-mails as you can, write a memo to Claudia, and staple all the missing e-mails to it."

I called technical support. The woman with whom I spoke explained that even though I had "deleted" the e-mails and emptied my virtual "trash" months earlier, the e-mails could still be retrieved from the hard drive. Nothing ever *really* disappears. The computer wizard walked me through a number of ballet steps to retrieve the e-mails from electronic storage, though I still don't know to this day if I was able to recover all of them.

As Don recommended, I wrote a memo to Claudia which referenced the two e-mails from me to De Pue, which Bellows possessed. The memo listed the three e-mails that survived in the PRAO file. It then listed, and attached copies of, 14 additional e-mails missing from the PRAO file that I had been able to retrieve from my computer. Finally, the memo asked Claudia to let me know if she wanted me to send Bellows the e-mails he did not have. I made a copy of the memo to preserve its contents, especially the attached e-mails, from later erasure. I placed the memo on her chair because she was not in her office.

I encountered Claudia on the elevator a couple of hours later. "Why weren't those e-mails in the file?" she snapped. It seemed like a rhetorical question.

I told her I had no idea. In my mind I was thinking, "*You* tell me, Claudia. Why *weren't* those e-mails in the file?"

"Now I have to explain why PRAO shouldn't look bad for not turning them over," she barked, exasperated. I found her comment puzzling because I thought her primary concern would be to ensure that the missing e-mails were sent to the Court as soon as possible.

"Do you want me to send them to Bellows?" I asked.

"No," she said firmly, "*I'll* handle it."

She never followed up with me about whether the e-mails were turned over to Bellows or to the Court. From contemporaneous and subsequent public statements made by the Department of Justice, it didn't sound as if they were.

During the next few weeks, Claudia came by my office as if nothing had happened, acting very solicitous and giving me job leads in other sections of the Department of Justice and other agencies of the government. She clearly wanted me gone.

The newspapers were filled with articles about the "American Taliban." They were all in agreement about one thing: the main legal issue in the case was whether statements Lindh made to FBI interrogators in Afghanistan should be admissible. Lindh's lawyers were contending that the government coerced him into speaking with FBI investigators by mistreating him and denying him access to a lawyer. They were right on target. A grand jury relied heavily on Lindh's statements when charging him with conspiring to kill Americans abroad and providing assistance to terrorist groups, including Osama bin Laden's al Qaeda network. If convicted, Lindh could face life in prison. My e-mails contained information about the interrogations during which Lindh made the most incriminating statements. The defense was seeking the e-mails, and I was not at all confident that the Justice Department had ever turned them over; in fact, I was quite certain that it had not.

On March 22, 2002, to the relief of both of us, my husband obtained a permanent job with the World Bank after being a consultant for a number of years. The position provided health insurance for our entire family, which allowed me to quit. I resigned that day.

Claudia threw me a big going away party and gave me a plaque thanking me for my distinguished service.

7. Disclosure

When I first tried to surmise the motivation for the cover-up, I thought that maybe Claudia was trying to protect the FBI, which by all accounts had been aggressive in its handling of Lindh. A photo went out around the world of him blindfolded, naked, and bound to a stretcher with duct tape. It was public news that he was left starving, cold, injured and sleep-deprived in a pitch-dark steel shipping container. So the missing e-mails, which documented the FBI's disregarding our advice and looking like a bunch of knuckle-dragging thugs, wouldn't have helped dispel this image.

But I later gained a more nuanced understanding of the cover-up. I came to see that our office's advice, and my e-mails in particular, directly contradicted the public position ultimately taken by the Attorney General, and someone desperately wanted to hide that PRAO had ever taken a contrary stance – namely, that Lindh was represented by counsel, could not be interrogated without his lawyer, and therefore the subsequent interrogation was unethical and could not be used in a criminal prosecution. Someone in the management chain of command, acting either alone or in concert with others, purged the file. That person or persons hoped to avoid detection of their duplicity by forcing me from the Department and trying to discredit me.

On April 8, 2002, within a month of discovering of the cover-up, I started a new job at Hawkins, Delafield & Wood, a private law firm, practicing affordable housing law, an area completely unrelated to my expertise and former position. This new job offered me a quick exit from an impossible work situation, the opportunity to do socially redeeming work, and a 25% salary increase to boot.

In May, the Lindh case was constantly in the news. There was no escaping it. And every journalist in print, radio and television seemed to be reading off the Justice Department script as the government released a steady stream of false, misleading and highly inflammatory information to the media. While getting dressed early one morning in June, I heard a broadcast on our local affiliate of National Public Radio, stating that the Justice Department had "never" taken the position that Lindh was entitled to counsel, a sentiment that I had heard expressed repeatedly during the preceding weeks. I knew this statement was not true. This assertion also indicated to me that the Justice Department had not turned over my e-mails to the court pursuant to the discovery order because I did not believe the Department would have the temerity to make public statements contradicted by its own court filings. This knowledge weighed heavily on me and turned me into a raging insomniac.

So I decided to blow the whistle. My decision came long before whistleblowing came into vogue, courtesy of TIME Magazine's 2002 "Persons of the Year." I was aware of the

Whistleblower Protection Act because, ironically, I wrote a memo on it when I worked at PRAO. The Act provides protection to federal government employees who expose government fraud, waste and abuse. It prohibits an agency official from taking an adverse personnel action against a former or current employee as a reprisal for any disclosure of information by an employee that the employee reasonably believes evidences a violation of any law, rule or regulation; gross mismanagement; or an abuse of authority. The situation I found myself in couldn't have been a more fitting example.

The language of the whistleblower law contemplates a disclosure to anyone inside or outside the agency in which the whistleblower is or was employed, including a reporter, a member of Congress, or an interest group representative. This interpretation is well-supported by case law. Interestingly – and somewhat counter-intuitively (because the logical place most employees would begin to disclose a problem is to their supervisors) – the U.S. Court of Appeals for the Federal Circuit held that complaints to a supervisor about the supervisor's own conduct are *not* disclosures covered by the Whistleblower Protection Act, but disclosures to the press are protected; thus, reporting misconduct up your chain-of-command doesn't count. The Supreme Court recently agreed that such on-the-job speech is not protected. The fact that I had confronted Claudia was not considered whistleblowing. It was not enough. I needed to ventilate the cover-up more publicly and outside of the Justice Department.

Fortunately, D.C.'s attorney ethics rules allow a government lawyer to reveal client confidences or secrets "when permitted or authorized by law." At least in theory, disclosures permitted by the Whistleblower Protection Act, even those that are not compelled, would not violate the ethics rules for government attorneys. The provision recognizes the "unique circumstances raised by attorney-client relationships within the government." There was also favorable precedent from the Clinton era, which held that a government agency could not invoke a privilege to prevent a government lawyer from providing evidence of the possible commission of criminal offenses within the government. In my circumstances, the Justice Department wanted to use the attorney-client privilege as both a sword and a shield, accusing me of breaching the privilege by revealing its misconduct, while hiding behind the privilege to commit illegal acts. But I know that there is no privilege to break the law. The attorney-client relationship cannot be used to further a crime.

I looked up the contact information for Michael Isikoff, *Newsweek's* veteran investigative reporter, who I had heard on the radio that morning toeing the Justice Department's party line. He broke the Paula Jones, Kathleen Willey and Monica Lewinsky stories, and much of what he uncovered led directly to the formal inquiry and ultimate impeachment of President Clinton. I certainly could not be accused of going to a flaming Democrat.

I went to Kinkos, an office and print center, and faxed the e-mails to him. I then went to see Mario, my surrogate therapist.

"Cut it all off," I said.

"Are you sure?" he asked.

"Yes," I said with a newfound certainty.

He tied my hair close to my scalp, braided it into a thick rope, cut it off, and placed it in a plastic bag. The other women in foils and curlers started clapping at my Sinéad O'Connor look. I donated my hair to "Locks of Love," which makes hairpieces for disadvantaged kids with medical hair loss. Cutting my hair was a symbolic act, the physical manifestation of my blowing the whistle. It was liberating. I was free. That night was the first time I was able to sleep soundly in months.

That was how I became *Newsweek's* source. I hate the term "leak" and "leaker" because what I really did was make a lawful *disclosure* as a *whistleblower* of my own e-mails, which would not have existed had I not resurrected them from the deep recesses of my computer's archives. But I won't get into the semantics because it is irrelevant to what followed.

Suffice it to say, I was unaware whether any of my e-mails had reached the court at the time I made the disclosure, and I had a more than reasonable belief that they had not. Until recently, if one were to review the docket sheet, it was like reading tea leaves because everything was under seal, meaning secret. One could

8. Hawkins, Delafield & Wood

In late June 2002, Agent Ron Powell of the Justice Department's Office of Inspector General phoned me at work to ask me questions about the *Newsweek* article. Little did I know that Agent Powell was about to become the Inspector Javert of my life, pursuing me relentlessly and obsessively, and making a normal life almost impossible.

Every major federal agency has an Office of Inspector General (OIG). A primary purpose of the office is to investigate reports of internal fraud, waste or abuse. The OIG staff is usually divided up between financial audits and investigations. While the office touts itself as independent, it really is not. In agencies like Justice, the Inspector General (IG) is nominated by the President and confirmed by the Senate. The IG reports to the head of the agency and serves at the pleasure of the President. In other words, if an IG is rocking the Administration's boat, he or she can be instantly removed. The IG's performance appraisal comes from the agency head, who also controls the issuance of awards and financial bonuses to the IG. As a consequence, OIGs are quite political in the selection of cases for investigation and the manner in which findings are cast.

However, Justice's Inspector General, Glenn Fine, had a good reputation – at least when it came to going after the "baby agencies" that the Department of Justice oversees: the FBI, INS, DEA, ATF, and Bureau of Prisons.

I had a quixotic view of the OIG as a kind of knight in shining armor – an outside, objective force riding over the hill to save me from the wrath of the Justice Department. My reliance on the OIG was misplaced. The OIG is a bureaucracy just like any other, with all the problems and limitations PRAO suffered. The IG controls the investigation. Often, the IG initiates a probe in response to a scandal first raised in the media. And often, the only real investigation that emanates from the IG centers not on the problem, but on the person who raised the problem. It is not unusual for the employee who made the report of misconduct to find him or herself the subject of the real investigation, and that is exactly what happened to me.

I cooperated initially with the IG, and tried to steer Agent Powell towards the issue of *why* someone would leak the e-mails, but he clearly had no intention of going there. All he cared about was plugging the leak. I felt as if he was trying to manipulate me into committing to dates and times I had already told him I couldn't remember; for example, he asked when I had eaten lunch with Don and another friend. I told him that it was sometime two weeks earlier, but I didn't remember the exact day. He then tried to deduce the date for me by calculating it based on imperfect and unreliable criteria. "Well, you know it wasn't Friday, and Monday wouldn't make sense, so you had lunch on Wednesday, right?"

71

"No," I said. "I already told you, I don't remember the exact day."

This same dance continued through a number of different songs. His tone grew increasingly invasive, accusatorial and antagonistic, and my answers became increasingly Clinton-esque, responding to only the exact question that was asked and not going beyond it. I felt that he was trying to paint me into a corner and get me to commit to things about which I was unsure. I would tell him I didn't know something, and then he would repeat the same information in concrete terms and ask me to agree.

"So you never called *Newsweek* or sent e-mail to *Newsweek* or faxed *Newsweek*. Records would never indicate that?" he demanded.

"I never made that denial. I could have returned a call to *Newsweek* or replied to an e-mail. Do you want to search my computer and phone records?"

"If it comes to that, we will," he warned ominously.

"Then I really have to go, Mr. Powell. I'll call you back."

Instead, I called a lawyer. I reached a friend of mine, Dan Jacobs, for advice. He had been the "John Doe" in the largest class action lawsuit ever brought by an employee against the Department of Justice, which he had won. Years earlier, he had also made disclosures of government wrongdoing, to which Assistant Attorney General Lois Schiffer issued orders prohibiting him from speaking to his own lawyers and made veiled threats of criminal

72

prosecution if he did so. He challenged that order and won a decision enjoining the prohibition.

Jacobs recommended that I speak with Rick Robinson (probably best known for representing former National Security Advisor John Poindexter in the Iran-Contra scandal) of Fulbright & Jaworski. The investigator left a number of messages, which luckily were memorialized on my voice mail. My friend also recommended that I create a contemporaneous record of my conversation with Agent Powell and transcribe Powell's message, which was one of the best pieces of advice I ever received.

Powell's message stated: "I just want to emphasize this is a voluntary interview and a voluntary conversation, so if you don't want to talk to me anymore, that's fine, that's your prerogative."

Two weeks later, on July 12, 2002, the Defense Department was apoplectic that its new policy on the torture of captives in the war on terrorism was going to be exposed. It was a Friday and Lindh's suppression hearing was scheduled for Monday. Defense made it clear to the Justice Department that it wanted the suppression hearing blocked. Michael Chertoff, the Assistant Attorney General for the Criminal Division (and now head of the Department of Homeland Security) who was overseeing all the Justice Department's terrorism prosecutions, had the prosecution team offer a deal: the serious charges against Lindh (e.g., terrorism, attempted murder, conspiracy to kill Americans, etc.) would be dropped and he would plead guilty to just two technical charges: providing aid to the Taliban government in violation of President Clinton's economic sanctions and carrying a weapon.

The first charge, that by serving as a soldier in Afghanistan he had violated anti-Taliban economic sanctions, was merely a regulatory infraction. The second charge, that he had carried a rifle and two grenades while serving as a volunteer soldier in the national army of Afghanistan, failed to note that Lindh had never fired his gun and surrendered his weapons to General Dostum long before encountering any Americans. The government dropped all 10 of its original terrorism charges.

Chertoff, at the Defense Department's insistence, demanded that Lindh sign a statement swearing he had "not been intentionally mistreated" by his U.S. captors and waiving any future right to claim mistreatment or torture. This plea effectively prevented early exposure of the Administration's policy of torture.

Lindh, whose attorneys dreaded a trial near the Pentagon on the first anniversary of 9/11, in the most conservative court district in the country, accepted the deal and its stiff twenty-year sentence. Chertoff sealed the plea agreement with a "special administrative measure" – a gag order – barring Lindh from discussing his experience for the duration of his sentence.

On the Monday morning that Lindh's suppression hearing was due to begin, in accordance with the deal negotiated over the weekend, Lindh pleaded guilty to the two relatively minor charges. The bombshell plea bargain, which startled even the judge, was announced before a packed courtroom awaiting the start of what was to be a crucial evidentiary hearing on whether statements Lindh made while in custody in Afghanistan – the ones I had advised against – could be used against him at his trial – which I had also advised against. The trial had been set to start the following month.

"Spotlight John" Ashcroft, as Richard Cohen calls him, hailed the Justice Department's anemic performance resulting in the surprise plea as "an important victory in America's war on terrorism." I think if it was a victory for anyone, however, it was a victory for Lindh. As Ashcroft had ominously noted six months earlier, "Walker Lindh could receive multiple life sentences, six additional 10-year sentences, plus 30 years." The twenty-year sentence was half of what he faced if convicted on the two minor charges alone. He could be released in 17 years. Lindh had won a future. It seemed like a good deal at the time.

As Jane Mayer of *The New Yorker* would later explain, "[I]n the Lindh case prosecutorial zeal appears to have weakened, rather than strengthened, the government's hand, contributing to a record of error that hastened the eventual settlement of the case on diminished charges."

Did I sink the government's case? No, the government sank its own case through its own missteps and misconduct. In the words spoken by Talleyrand two centuries ago: Above all, not too much zeal.

Little did I realize that I had unleashed the full force of the entire Executive Branch.

In a 50-page Justice Department memo dated August 1, 2002 – obtained nearly two years later by the *Washington Post* and soon known popularly as the "torture memo" – Bybee of Justice's Office of Legal Counsel advised White House Counsel Gonzales that torturing al Qaeda terrorists detained abroad "may be justified," and that international laws against torture "may be unconstitutional if applied to interrogations" conducted in the war on terrorism. The legal opinion, titled "Standards of Conduct for Interrogation," was not discussed or shared with the U.S. Joint Chiefs of Staff, the military's most senior leaders, or the State Department. (The Justice Department had learned its lesson back in the winter.)

The memo drew a sharp distinction between torture, "an egregious, extreme act," and the more vague "cruel, inhuman or degrading treatment" of detainees. According to the Justice Department, inflicting moderate or fleeting pain does not constitute torture; instead, *physical* torture "must be equivalent in intensity to the pain accompanying serious physical injury, such as organ failure, impairment of bodily function, or even death." For a cruel or inhuman technique to rise to the level of *psychological* torture, the mental harm must last "months or even years."

Even under the Justice Department's extreme definition, the United States still committed torture at its detention facilities. That Justice Department officials knew that their proposal was legally shaky comes across in the memo's suggestion that "necessity or self-defense could provide justifications that would eliminate any criminal liability." Never mind that if Rwanda or the former Yugoslavia made these arguments in front of a war crimes tribunal, they would be laughed right out of court.

After the memo leaked, President Bush, with his selective amnesia, said that he could not remember whether he had seen it – as if a memo on such an important issue would not make a lasting impression. The Justice Department responded to the leak by disavowing the memo, calling parts of it overbroad and irrelevant, and promising that it would be reviewed, rewritten and replaced by a new memo more carefully addressing the question of proper interrogation techniques for al Qaeda and Taliban detainees. But the White House and Justice Department's face-saving public relations effort was nothing more than a transparent attempt at damage control to contain the diplomatic and political backlash caused by U.S. torture. Their repudiation of the memo was not at all credible and the rejected version was not replaced by the intransigent Administration for another six months.

Although the memo was not related to questions about the handling of detainees at Guantánamo Bay or in Iraq, it nonetheless lay the groundwork for the government's overall thinking about interrogations of terror detainees captured elsewhere. While it only addressed the treatment of al Qaeda detainees in CIA custody, it provided the legal underpinnings for subsequent abuses of prisoners in Afghanistan and Iraq, and the Defense Department had already relied on it in crafting a much longer and more inflammatory March 2003 classified Pentagon report examining the logistical, policy and legal issues associated with interrogating the detainees at Guantánamo Bay, Cuba.

Obviously, "exercising my prerogative" (in the words of Agent Powell) to decline speaking with him further was *not* fine because on August 15th, he called my new firm and told the receptionist, the office manager and a partner that he was conducting a "criminal investigation" of me and that the firm had "just hired a criminal." I note here that I have never received a subject or target letter, never been named a suspect (or even a "person of interest," Bush-speak for branding you guilty when they don't have enough evidence to bring a real case), never been arrested, and never been criminally charged, prosecuted or convicted. When the investigator requested phone and fax records, the partner referred him to a managing partner in Hawkins' New York office, W. Cullen MacDonald. Suffice it to say, the investigator's inflammatory contact with over half the people in my small D.C. office excited much anxiety on the part of my law firm. And it certainly intimidated and rattled me.

Two weeks later, I got a letter from Justice's Office of Professional Responsibility (OPR), the internal disciplinary component, requesting information about a case I was involved in that was unrelated to the Lindh case. Rick, my attorney, thought it might be a backdoor way of talking to me about the Lindh matter, or retaliation for my refusal to speak to the IG or for embarrassing PRAO. Working at the Department of Justice had become a Kafkaesque nightmare from which I could not awake. They were trying to ruin my career. I knew OPR was being egged on by PRAO. Their directors were friends. How much damage could one vengeful institution inflict on me? The Department's incessant harassment knew no bounds, and these calls to my new firm were only the beginning.

Agent Powell continued to hound anyone who had the misfortune of being associated with me. I learned from Don Mackay that Powell insisted on knowing when Don, Jim and I had lunch. Powell said, "Was it right after Jim said that Isikoff contacted him that Jesselyn said that she talked to him?"

"Jesselyn never said that at all," Don insisted, correctly. "You're putting words in my mouth."

Then Agent Powell went back and re-interviewed Jim. Jim later told Don, "He had me coming and going. He was trying to convince me that Jesselyn told us she spoke to Isikoff. I'm 84 and my memory is still intact, but he was really confusing me, talking me in circles."

I felt just awful that my friends were paying a price for associating with me. I didn't tell my secret to anyone, including my husband, for precisely that reason: I wanted to give them plausible deniability. I didn't want my colleagues, friends or family dragged into this quagmire, or worse, to be in a position where they would have to implicate me. I wanted them to be able to say honestly that we had never discussed it.

The anniversary of September 11th came and went. The Jewish new year followed shortly after, and again, I tried to draw strength from the liturgy: "O Source of mercy, give us the grace to show forbearance of those who offend against us. When the wrongs and injustices of others wound us, may our hearts not despair of human good. May no trial, however severe, embitter our souls and destroy our trust."

I wouldn't go so far as to say I was wounded, despairing, embittered, and destroyed. I was more hurt, unsure, angry and worried.

The prayer continued: "When beset by trouble and sorrow, our mothers and fathers put on the armor of faith and fortitude. May we too find strength to meet adversity with quiet courage and unshaken will. Help us to understand that injustice and hate will not forever afflict the human race; that righteousness and mercy will triumph in the end." The words applied to my personal situation and to the ongoing terrorism more generally.

Luckily, at the annual firm dinner, I met Cullen MacDonald in person and he was very supportive and reassuring.

"Everyone who works for the government gets investigated at one point or another," he joked. "It's almost a rite of passage inside the Beltway. It builds thick skin."

My husband and I ended up in assigned seating across from him at dinner, whether by design or coincidence, and enjoyed hours of pleasant conversation with this affable and very paternal man.

After a month of the government leaning on him, however, MacDonald changed his tune. On October 1st, he wrote a terse e-mail to my attorney "at the instruction of our firm's Management Committee to apprise you of the circumstantial evidence presently under consideration by the Inspector General of the Department of Justice." He attached an outline of the "evidence," which basically documented Isikoff's calling and reaching my voice mail four times, and my speaking with him twice and sending him a fax.

Could the Justice Department have obtained an order for a pen register, which identifies all outgoing numbers called by a given telephone, on Isikoff? Could it have secured an order for a trap-and-trace device, which identifies the phone numbers of incoming callers, on me?

Post-Watergate regulations adopted by the Department of Justice establish a clear procedure for subpoenaing a journalist's phone records. First, the government must take all other reasonable steps to obtain the information sought, before reporters are subpoenaed or approached in an investigation. Second, once the government has exhausted all other reasonable steps, the department can seek a subpoena of the reporter's phone records from a court, but must notify the reporter so that he or she may contest the request. Third, only under extraordinary circumstances, and with the direct authorization of the Attorney General, can federal agents subpoena a reporter's records from the phone company without the reporter's knowledge, but the agents must inform the reporter within 45 days that they have done so.

These guidelines were not followed in my case. It's a mystery that is still unsolved today, but one that certainly haunts journalists. Douglas McCollam wrote an article for the *Columbia Journalism Review* on my "creepy" situation, appropriately titled, "Who's Tracking Your Calls? And How Far Will the Department of Justice Go To Burn a Leaker?" He didn't find the answer, but issued an important warning that I hope both journalists and whistleblowers will heed: "The government got a record of Isikoff's calls to an important source on an important story, without either party's knowing about it. It's a quick lesson on how far an irate government may go to burn your source. So remember, even on a local line, let's be careful out there."

I frantically called Isikoff. "I need a copy of the fax I sent you from Hawkins or else I'm going to be fired."

"I can't just hand it over it to you," he said. "Have your attorney call me about it."

So I paid Rick $200 to pick up the phone and convince Isikoff to send it. Luckily, the "smoking fax," which was just my law review article, matched the time, date and duration of the fax in the IG's flimsy arsenal of "evidence" with which Hawkins confronted me. I had not sent secret government documents from the firm. It was just my boring scholarship.

Someday I should write a "how-to" guide for potential whistleblowers: forget leaking anonymously, forget going to the papers, go straight to Congress, do not pass go, do not collect any money from anybody, hold your own press conference, shout it from the rooftops. Speak only on pay phones or throw-away cell phones, but never your home or office phone. Keep copious records and a daily diary of relevant information. Memorialize conversations in writing. Maintain a separate set of documents outside of work in a safe place. Your chances of success will likely depend on how powerful a paper trail you produce. But that's a whole other book.

Regardless of whether the Justice Department traced Isikoff's calls and shared the results with Hawkins, or traced Hawkins' calls, the thing that was most disturbing was how "Big Brother" it all seemed. In violation of its own internal regulations, the Department of Justice had shared details and evidence of an ongoing federal investigation with my private employer, impugned the reputation of an uncharged third party (me), and was using my employer as an instrument to accomplish what it otherwise could not.

Why was I surprised? In the Lindh case, numerous Department protocols were violated. In the investigation of the anthrax "person of interest," Dr. Steven Hatfill, which was running concurrent to the investigation of me, the Department similarly violated its own regulations, engaging in character assassination instead of criminal charge, defamation instead of due process, and innuendo instead of evidence. It's what the government does when it can't make a case. Ask Richard Jewell or Wen Ho Lee, or more recently, Brandon Mayfield, a Portland area lawyer whose fingerprint was erroneously identified with "100 percent" certainty on a bag of detonators found near the site of a terror attack on a train station in Madrid. Numerous U.S. government leaks condemned Mayfield in the court of public opinion because he is a Muslim convert, married an Egyptian-born woman, worships at a mosque, spoke with an Islamic charity, and represented a convicted terrorism conspirator in an unrelated child custody case. It was the Spanish authorities that exonerated him, not the U.S. His case shows how an impressive-looking condemnation can be built entirely on sand.

Steven Hatfill's eventual lawsuit against the government devoted an entire paragraph to the hypocrisy of the Department's tactics with regard to the two of us:

> [The Justice Department's] half-hearted effort to identify the source of these defamatory leaks [about Hatfill] stands in stark contrast to the enormous resources DOJ has brought to bear in other cases in which information that the DOJ considers embarrassing has

been leaked to the press. The disparate treatment makes one thing clear: Leaks that embarrass the DOJ are treated seriously and lead to criminal referrals (as in the case of DOJ employee Jesselyn Radack), while leaks the DOJ and FBI view as helpful (by placing the organizations in a good light) are ignored.

The Bush Administration leaks like a sieve when it suits their needs.

MacDonald e-mailed that the Management Committee was inclined to ask for my resignation. The Justice Department was leaning on them heavily, and Hawkins was clearly playing hardball with me. MacDonald was unapologetic about the firm's willingness to act as an agent of the government. My immediate supervisors, Tony Freedman and John McNally, both told me that many people on the Management Committee thought that MacDonald's tone in the e-mail was too harsh.

I had worked for Hawkins, Delafield & Wood for six months and had never given them any reason to doubt my safeguarding of attorney-client privileged and confidential information. I was told that I could make personal phone calls and occasional use of the fax machine, and was even provided with a code for doing so.

A few days later, I was still dodging bullets. I ran into MacDonald skulking around our small D.C. branch (he normally worked out of the home office in New York). He looked very sheepish, as if I had caught him with his hand in the cookie jar, or nosing around my office to be more exact.

"You should know that at this very moment, Agent Powell is interviewing your boss and may be walking around here," he said, seeming very flustered. Then his tone grew more ominous. "The investigator is near the end of his investigation and is ready to *take action.*"

As visions flashed through my mind of the police breaking down my door and forcing me to do the perp walk in front of the neighborhood soccer moms, I started to panic. To say that I was scared doesn't capture the depth of my fear.

That night, we went to "family swim" at the local high school pool to try to take my mind off things at work. My husband tried to reassure me. "You're pregnant! That's why you're so emotional. I just know it. And look how buoyant you are!"

I woke up the next morning with my nightgown soaked in blood and burst into tears.

My lawyer informed my firm in no uncertain terms that I was a federal whistleblower, and proved – by producing the fax cover sheet with the date, time and length of transmission – that the damning fax the IG claimed was my "leaking secret government documents" from my law firm was nothing more than my sending Isikoff a copy of the law review article I had written. He assured the Management Committee that I neither used the firm's facilities to provide government materials to a member of the press, nor engaged in any other act that violates the ethical obligations of members of the bar; in fact, I provided information to the IG while simply protecting my own legal and constitutional rights to be free from further harassment and retaliation by the government.

On the same day, my attorney sent a letter to the IG spelling out my allegations in no uncertain terms: "While Ms. Radack worked at PRAO, she took several steps to thwart efforts by others within that office to conceal material regarding the Lindh case from the court. As a result of those actions, she was subjected to a series of unlawful, retaliatory acts, all in violation of [the Whistleblower Protection Act]. We believe that the actions of Special Agent Powell are intended to further that retaliation against Ms. Radack by interfering with her current employment and otherwise besmirching her reputation."

On October 11, 2002, officers at the Guantánamo prison camp asked their superiors for permission to use harsher interrogation methods against inmates. Major General Michael E. Dunlavey, the commanding general at the Guantánamo Bay facility, asked his commander, General James T. Hill, chief of the U.S. Southern Command, to approve the use of threats "to convince the detainee that death or severely painful consequences are imminent for him and/or his family," "a wet towel and dripping water to induce the misperception of suffocation," stress positions, "exposure to cold weather or water," and menacing dogs. Dunlavey's legal advisor had reviewed these techniques and deemed them legal under the Geneva Conventions "so long as there is an important governmental objective" and the tactics are not used "for the purpose of causing harm or with the intent to cause prolonged" mental or physical suffering. (When suffocation by water was used by the Pinochet dictatorship in Chile, the State Department didn't hesitate to call it torture.)

That same day, the government filed an *ex parte* and sealed document in the Lindh matter that "relates solely to the unauthorized disclosure of certain documents filed in this case by persons other than the defendant or members of the defense team." That must have been what Cullen MacDonald was cryptically referring to. It was the "leak report." It all should have ended right there. Just like it should have ended after Lindh pleaded guilty. There are so many occasions on which it should have ended.

On October 25, 2002, Dunlavey's commander, General Hill, expressed unease with the legal advisor's assessment of the new interrogation techniques and asked the chairman of the Joint Chiefs of Staff, General Richard B. Myers, for guidance. "I am uncertain whether all the techniques . . . are legal under U.S. law, given the absence of judicial interpretation of the U.S. torture statute. I am particularly troubled by the use of implied or express threats of death of the detainee and his family."

9. The Sniper

Two weeks later, the Management Committee gave me an affidavit stating that I had not leaked my e-mail to *Newsweek*, and told me in Johnnie Cochran-esque terms to "sign or resign." Once again I found myself in the middle of the night wide-awake with worry about what to do. I wanted to cry, but was too angry. If anyone had told me a year before that the government would be *lying* to my private employer and trying to destroy me professionally, I never would have believed it.

But now I was a caged bird – afraid to go to the grocery store for fear of running into former PRAO colleagues who lived nearby, afraid to leave my office for fear of running into *anyone* from the Department of Justice (it was only a block away), afraid to talk to anyone (because they would be interrogated afterward), afraid to go to work (because I might get fired that day), afraid to go to sleep (because I'd have nightmares about this), afraid to wake up (because of whatever torment the day would bring), and afraid of the years this would rob from my life.

Rick Robinson recommended that I consult an employment attorney, so I retained one of D.C.'s top guns, Mona Lyons, of Clifford, Lyons & Garde. She's a tough-as-nails attorney with a heart of gold, a great sense of humor, and a brilliant mind. I sent her firm all of Rick's correspondence to give them a flavor of what was going on. They asked if I could meet in person. When I got there, Mona, another partner, and an associate spoke with me for nearly two hours. I will never forget it. We sat around a large conference table brainstorming. They were all amazing and Mona totally deserved her ranking among *Washingtonian Magazine*'s top 50 lawyers.

It was the first time I felt not only supported in what I had done, but also *wronged* by what had followed. The experience with them legitimized my feeling of being unceremoniously railroaded by the Department of Justice, and now by my law firm. My case presented a number of novel issues. There was the post-employment retaliation by my former employer (the Justice Department) via my new employer (Hawkins). There was the public policy exception to the employment-at-will doctrine, which I would seemingly fit into as a whistleblower – a fact about which Rick had done an excellent job putting the firm on notice. Therefore, to fire me for *that reason* is unlawful because public policy favors blowing the whistle and it was not my performance with which Hawkins had a problem.

We decided to try to put the pin back in the grenade. Because of the IG's ongoing investigation of the underlying issues, and its need to investigate *my* whistleblower claims, and because my conduct was protected by law and public policy, I did not sign the affidavit. Plus, it was clear that Hawkins wanted me to execute the affidavit for ulterior reasons, namely for the benefit of the government, which exhibited no

90

interest whatsoever in investigating the underlying cover-up that had actually occurred.

By sick coincidence, a serial sniper was terrorizing our region. Eleven people had been shot in the sniper attacks since October 2nd, and nine had died. The most recent shooting was at the Home Depot hardware store that was practically our second home. The kids had no outdoor recess or gym and their field trips were cancelled.

So, in a parallel universe, some killer was literally hunting people in our neighborhood. And on a personal level, I felt stalked by the Justice Department, which was going after me with both barrels and an endless supply of artillery and ammunition. I felt as if the rapacious Department would go to the ends of the earth to destroy me. There was no visible end in sight. If they were trying to stop me from practicing law, trying to intimidate me and trying to break me, then they were succeeding.

I was running on fumes, holding it together with gum and a shoestring. The serial sniper shot two more people. But the anxiety I (and the rest of the D.C. metropolitan area) felt over the serial sniper was paralleled by the anxiety I felt waiting to hear from the Management Committee. Waiting for the ax to fall was giving me *agita* – that special kind of existential dyspepsia of the soul. It had a huge effect on my morale, my health, my very core. As an adult, the feeling of dread was no different from when I was five. It put me back on the couch in the den of my childhood, learning that my parents were separated but not yet divorced.

91

On October 24, 2002, police caught the snipers who had paralyzed the region that month. "Aren't you relieved?" a Hawkins colleague e-mailed me.

Yes, I was relieved momentarily, until I received an e-mail from Cullen MacDonald telling me that the Management Committee was placing me on a leave of absence starting the following day. The heavy-handed tactic of placing me on leave and giving me one day's notice again took me by surprise. My hands grew ice cold, I started shaking, and became short of breath. I felt like I needed to vomit. Oddly enough, I still felt determined to finish my work. For having professed doubts about my trustworthiness, the firm continued to give me substantive assignments and attorney-client matters to handle up until the minute I left. I even worked late on my last day.

On November 4, 2002, Major General Miller took command of the Guantánamo prison camp with a mandate to get more and better information from the prisoners. He ran a much tighter ship and placed a premium on clarifying the responsibilities of his subordinates. Two days later, Patrick F. Philbin, a deputy in the Justice Department's Office of Legal Counsel, laid out in a confidential 35-page memorandum to White House Counsel Gonzales, the legal basis for the Administration's approach to military tribunals. The memo said that the President has "inherent authority," as commander in chief, to establish military tribunals without Congressional authorization, and that the attacks of September 11th were "plainly sufficient" to warrant applying the laws of war. It suggested that the White House could apply international law selectively and that trying terrorists under the laws of war "does not mean that terrorists will receive the protections of the Geneva Conventions."

The memo opened a debate that would later divide the Administration.

My attorney and I met with MacDonald a week later, which turned out to be a wasted trip to New York and an exercise in futility and frustration. MacDonald was not so kindly and paternal after all, but a loose canon with a Napoleonic complex – condescending, rude and completely ignorant of employment law generally and whistleblower law in particular. He kept saying that he wanted to explore "option enlarging" strategies, which sounded like bad business school jargon, but what he really wanted to know were the salacious details of what happened in the Lindh affair. This approach put me in an impossible situation because it would have entailed violating the very attorney-client privilege I was being accused by the Justice Department of breaching. He told me unambiguously, "All the D.C. partners love your work." But he also said that even if I made a valid disclosure under the Whistleblower Protection Act, he disagreed with my "judgment." Again, I was damned if I told all, and damned if I didn't.

Moreover, Hawkins was really tying my hands. I was not getting paid, but I couldn't apply for unemployment benefits because I was technically still employed there. They were trying to force a resignation. I refused to give in.

"Mommy, are you going to die?" my two-year-old asked me one evening.

"Goodness no, Sam! Why would you ask such an awful thing?" I ventured, fearing that in his toddler mind he somehow grasped that I had MS.

"Because I heard you tell Anna's mom that you were going to be fired."

Sam was equating being "fired" with being "shot," a term that was all over the news because of the snipers. It was the very literal way that toddlers often interpret the world. But it broke my heart that the work situation had trickled down to my kids in this kind of way.

Hawkins paid me for one month. Without the courtesy of giving me any notice, they cut off my pay the next month, even though their attorney, Betsy Plevan, insisted to Mona that no such decision had been reached. Plevan asked if I would agree to a suspension without pay on a Tuesday, but the letter cutting off my pay was postmarked Monday. As an equal breadwinner for my family, this was a double-whammy. I was no longer pulling in income, and at the same time racking up legal bills.

In a Pentagon memo dated November 27, 2002, the Defense Department's chief lawyer, Haynes, recommended that Rumsfeld approve the use of 14 interrogation techniques on detainees at Guantánamo Bay, such as yelling at prisoners during questioning and using "stress positions," like standing for up to four hours. Haynes also recommended approval of one technique among the harsher methods requested by U.S. military authorities at Guantánamo: the use of "mild, non-injurious physical contact such as grabbing, poking in the chest with the finger and light pushing." However, he cautioned moderation, noting that while certain techniques were available as a matter of policy, blanket approval was not warranted at the time.

When Rumsfeld read Haynes' memo, he added a sarcastic handwritten note at the bottom: "I stand for 8-10 hours a day. Why is standing limited to 4 hours?" Rumsfeld issued an order allowing harsh interrogation techniques at Guantánamo. They included forcing prisoners into "stress positions," interrogating them for 20 hours at a time, stripping them, menacing them with dogs, forcing them to wear hoods during transportation and interrogation, and forcibly shaving their heads and beards. Vice President Dick Cheney would later tell CNN that the detainees were well treated, well fed, and "living in the tropics."

The unemployment rate that December was the highest it had been in nine years, and I was now effectively part of it. Rick drafted a letter to the IG, whom we hadn't heard from in over two months, asking them to inform us as soon as possible of what steps their office intended to take with respect to the whistleblower matters we raised. Rick's letter also noted that we learned that the IG had filed its leak report. "This filing, coupled with the lack of any response to Ms. Radack's allegations, would seem to suggest that the investigation regarding the Lindh matter has concluded."

Meanwhile, Cullen MacDonald sent Rick an e-mail: "Last week you left word on my voice mail that you were trying to learn the status of the IG's investigation to see if the filing of its report with the court allowed you to have your client become more cooperative and forthcoming with the Management Committee. The ball is in her court."

Rick pointed out that he had written the IG twice and suspected that the IG would be much more forthcoming in responding to an inquiry from MacDonald since MacDonald was the one helping the IG with its investigation. It was ridiculous that Hawkins was trying to put the onus on *us* to determine the status of the government's investigation when *Hawkins* was the one playing footsie with the Justice Department.

Still, Hawkins continued to insist that *we* should be doing more in the way of bringing "this" to a close. Their attorney asked what Rick thought the Committee should do. He said they should let me come back to work because I had provided them with an explanation of my contacts with Isikoff from the office and shown that I was correct on the law.

Hawkins said that they were still not convinced that the ethics rules allowed a non-compulsory disclosure. Rick said they were wrong and that we had addressed this point *ad nauseam* in our last letter and that the D.C. ethics rules on this were clear. Hawkins replied that the firm was still entitled to know how I "exercised my judgment" even if there was no ethical violation. The law firm appeared to be projecting *its* ethical shortcomings onto me.

Rick suspected that the Management Committee was not going along with MacDonald's recommendations and may have wished to be more accommodating than MacDonald had been.

By the end of December, the firm was still in the same position that it had been in at the beginning of the month, when their lawyer had promised a decision *that week*. The parties' stances had not changed. Hawkins needed to return me to work, put me back on paid leave, or fire me. If not, after a certain date, I could construe their actions as a constructive discharge and seek unemployment benefits, and maybe eventually sue for back pay.

The firm kept moving the target. Whenever I answered their questions, provided legal authority, or attended their kangaroo meetings, they came up with new and different requirements.

Rick received another missive from MacDonald. It was the second time MacDonald stated my "disclosure of privileged communications to the news media" as if it were a foregone conclusion. Like the IG, the Management Committee was trying to put words in my mouth – the reason I terminated my initial cooperation with the IG. To be clear, I had told the Management Committee only that I engaged in conduct protected by the Whistleblower Protection Act. I didn't tell them what that conduct entailed. As a grand favor, Hawkins said it was "allowing" me to stay on unpaid leave for two more months. It was like Claudia saying that she would hold the spiteful performance evaluation in abeyance until I found another job. Don't do me any favors.

Three women whistleblowers in high-profile cases were named as "Persons of the Year" for 2002 by TIME Magazine. I don't know if I agree with the gendered construction of whistleblowing that the media endorsed. I am not a biological essentialist who embraces the valorization of difference. In my case, the bad actors included just as many women as men, and women had certainly not cornered the market on integrity. But the TIME article still emboldened me. Sherron Watkins, Coleen Rowley and Cynthia Cooper's advice was to stand up and do the right thing. It provided a glimmer of light after a low point on the roller coaster created by the law firm's latest salvo.

Upon Rick's advice, I spoke with Doug Hartnett of the Government Accountability Project on December 30, 2002. MacDonald called Rick that night, pressuring Rick to call the IG and telling Rick how to do his job. It was almost as if MacDonald were scared of the IG.

Dan and I met with Mona Lyons on New Year's Eve. She agreed that I shouldn't resign, but she also thought that I should start looking for another job. Under D.C. law, I had been constructively discharged and she said I should try to seek unemployment compensation. It would have been hard to initiate a civil action against Hawkins because I'd have to give them in discovery the information that I had been refusing to provide.

Dan, Rick and I met with Tom Devine and Doug Hartnett of the Government Accountability Project the next day. They were very helpful and cleverly suggested that I tell MacDonald that if *he* got a waiver from the Justice Department (which would never happen), then I'd tell him anything and everything he wanted to know about the Lindh case. They also noted that the Justice Department was ignoring *notice* that the agency had been cheating. The upshot of the meeting was that I needed to shift the spotlight off of myself and shine it onto Justice's dark propaganda. I was dealing with an Administration that was masterful at distractions, distortions and changing the subject.

I updated my resume and started the arduous process of looking for another job. I went to the D.C. Department of Employment Service Office of Unemployment Compensation and applied for benefits, a very humbling experience. I became a card-carrying member of the ACLU. I e-mailed my law school mentors. I took the first baby steps in moving forward.

But it was only hours before the Justice Department stuck a leg in my path to trip me up.

At the end of the day on January 7, 2003, I returned a call from Rick. He said that Glenn Fine, the Inspector General himself, had called him with two pieces of bad news. The IG "looked into it" (my whistleblower allegations), and they "were not going to pursue it." My immediate

99

reaction was that they didn't look very deeply. They didn't even bother to ask *me*, the whistleblower, what happened. They didn't bother to interview the complainant!

The second piece of bad news, to add insult to injury, was that there was an open criminal investigation of *me* (for what, the IG would not specify) and that they decided to refer it to Stuart Nash in the D.C. U.S. Attorney's Office for prosecution. I had friends in that office. It was all so through-the-looking-glass.

Rick said the criminal matter was a dog case and not to lose sleep over it, but how could I not? I started a law review article during my restless nights and finished it in less than a week. Lending credence to the adage that the personal is political, the article argued that blowing the whistle is an exception to the ethics rule governing confidentiality, especially in light of the fact that the rule was amended in 2002 to add a new exception to confidentiality in order "to comply with other law." The Whistleblower Protection Act, I argued, is precisely the kind of "other law" that should be recognized. I submitted it exclusively to *The Georgetown Journal of Legal Ethics*, which I learned was doing a symposium issue on whistleblowers. I did not want my article placed anywhere else, so I put all of my eggs in one basket and luckily it was accepted.

In a January 15th memo to the Pentagon's general counsel, Rumsfeld asked Haynes to convene a working group to consider legal, policy and operational issues relating to interrogations of detainees held by the U.S.

military in the war on terrorism. His decision was prompted at least in part by objections raised by some military lawyers who felt that the techniques approved for use at Guantánamo Bay might go too far. That same day, in another memo to the head of the U.S. Southern Command, Rumsfeld rescinded his December 2nd approval of some interrogation techniques for Guantánamo Bay. The memo allowed commanders to seek Rumsfeld's direct approval to use the tougher methods if they were "warranted in an individual case," and referenced the other memo to Haynes.

That same day, Hawkins' attorney called Rick. It was a very odd conversation, as if Hawkins had taken English lessons from Bush on how to speak in double negatives. The upshot was that Hawkins didn't want me *not* to be their employee. They went back and forth on the same old issues – Hawkins' "right" to know all of the details about Lindh and my inability to tell them. Rick told Hawkins that I wanted back pay and pay for the rest of the year if they wanted a release from a lawsuit. I was surprised they still wanted me to work for them at all. It was probably more that they didn't want to get sued.

Rick called Stuart Nash at the D.C. U.S. Attorney's Office. He wasn't doing much with the case. "It's not on the back burner, but it's not on the front burner, either," he said.

Nash said he wasn't ready to talk about possible charges, but that he would let Rick know if he decided to go forward *and* if he decided not to, which was generous of him. I

101

think he saw it for the witch-hunt that it was. In the biggest surprise, the IG had *not* given Nash our letters claiming whistleblower protection. I hate to sound like a conspiracy theorist, but it seemed at best a sloppy oversight and, at worst, another cover-up. The fact that I was a whistleblower was information that could be exculpatory to any charge that Nash might bring. So much for the criminal justice system, where investigations must have a clear objective and the information collected – and the means by which it is acquired – must ultimately be shared with the accused and tested in open court.

Rick said maybe it was time to go to a member of the press. Mona agreed.

10. Muckraker Jane

On January 17, 2003, the Pentagon's Haynes designated the general counsel for the Air Force to head the working group that Rumsfeld requested in one of his January 15th memos.

President Bush may not have known the particulars of American-led torture, but his public statements continued to suggest that he had a good idea. "All told, more than 3,000 suspected terrorists have been arrested in many countries," he boasted in his State of the Union address on January 28, 2003. "Many others have met a different fate. Let's put it this way — they are no longer a problem . . ."

On February 4th, Jane Mayer of *The New Yorker* literally showed up on my doorstep. I was at the grocery store, but she left a message neatly penned on notebook paper:

> *Dear Jesselyn –*
> *I am really sorry to bother you like this, but I couldn't get a phone number to call. I'm writing for* The New Yorker *magazine, currently looking back at the Lindh-Walker case, and I hoped to interview you about it either on or off the record. It seems your concerns were prescient,*

so I was interested in your
perspective . . .
Again, sorry for the imposition,
but it's a serious subject and I
wanted to try to reach you.

All the best,
Jane Mayer

As if I didn't know who she was! As if *The New Yorker* wasn't the only magazine to which I subscribed! As if I had not been aching for a godsend like this to fall into my lap. It was heartening to know that someone, especially an investigative reporter of Jane Mayer's caliber, was giving the John Walker Lindh matter a closer look.

My attorneys and I had been discussing "going public," and Jane Mayer presented the perfect opportunity. She had been researching the article for months and her focus was on government overreaching in the Lindh case. Her note felt like divine intervention.

Hawkins, after continually ignoring our request that they respond to my severance proposal, called Rick back immediately when they got wind of the forthcoming article. Their attorney hit the roof. She was furious and said I couldn't talk about anything having to do with Hawkins – namely, their treatment of me. Rick assured her that I would not discuss client matters, but that I had every right to discuss Hawkins' ugly conduct. Hawkins was nervous because they were easily recognizable to *New*

Yorker readers as the firm of famous novelist Louis Auchincloss.

Hawkins' attorney called Mona, saying that she "thought it was time for the employment lawyers to talk." Mona called her back to reiterate our position that they needed to respond to our severance proposal and that they couldn't stop me from talking to the press about the terms and conditions of my employment.

During this time, a draft version of the Patriot Act II (the "Domestic Security Enhancement Act of 2003") leaked from the Justice Department. It took the Patriot Act's civil liberties deprivations even further. It provided for the creation of a DNA database of terrorism suspects and their associates, the power to wiretap Americans for fifteen days without a court order after terrorist attacks, and the ability to block bail for terrorism suspects, make secret arrests, expand the federal death penalty to convicted terrorists, and strip the American citizenship of anyone who helped an organization the Attorney General deems "terrorist." Chuck Lewis of the Center for Public Integrity, to which the legislation was leaked, praised the "leaker" as a patriot and a hero who would be professionally ruined. I knew how correct he was.

Hawkins' lawyer left a voice mail message for Rick to see if they could move things forward. Basically, she said the firm would propose two months' severance conditioned on a "non-disparagement" agreement. She said she didn't think the firm had a lot of flexibility, which was

105

obviously bluster, but would try to get them to do a little better if Rick could get me closer to two months' severance.

In mid-February I was awarded unemployment compensation benefits. It wasn't much, but enough to buy groceries and gas for the week.

Hawkins called Rick to say that they didn't believe I could "control any journalist." Rick, with Mona's help, sent a crisp e-mail saying that I had control over whether the firm would be identified in *The New Yorker*, and that I obviously had complete control over whether I spoke to any other news outlets.

Rick also got a voice mail from Nash at the U.S. Attorney's Office, which said that Nash expected to be in a position to tell Rick what he planned to do with the case in the next two to three weeks, but that he couldn't provide additional details. It was getting ridiculous. A fundamental component of due process is the right to confront one's accusers. It's founded on the premise that the truth is most likely to emerge in an adversarial proceeding, where the accused, who is in the best position to defend herself, can confront the sources of evidence against her, and can challenge their veracity, reveal their bias, and catch them in contradiction. But in my situation, it felt like the usual presumption was reversed. I was guilty until proven innocent.

Cullen MacDonald sent Rick a threatening and desperate e-mail:

> Because the firm would consider any mention of its name in a nationwide publication concerning your client...

to be harmful to its reputation, it hereby requests that she exercise the power... she has to keep our name out of it. It is indisputable that any employee willfully causing disparaging publicity about his or her employer would be subject to immediate discharge.

However, Hawkins, Delafield & Wood had already constructively discharged me. Plus, I had no need or desire to disparage Hawkins. I would simply tell the truth. The fact that they were ashamed of their conduct spoke for itself. Private entities need to be held accountable, especially in this Orwellian era of the inaptly-named Patriot Act, for acting as agents of the government in a way that forces employees to check their constitutional rights at the door.

Rick strategized with Mona and wrote back:

First, I had thought I had made clear that Ms. Radack was willing to exercise her ability to keep the firm's name out of the upcoming *New Yorker* article only as part of an overall severance agreement. Second, we do not believe that the firm is treating Ms. Radack as an employee or that a recitation of the facts regarding the firm's treatment of an employee can provide cause for termination of the employee . . .

A week later, I received a "Notice of In-Person Hearing." Hawkins had filed an appeal of the determination that granted me unemployment compensation – a determination that specifically found that I was "not discharged for misconduct." It was unclear how much the government was pulling Hawkins' strings, but Hawkins was certainly acting as vindictively as the government.

As the office of unemployment compensation identified the issues, Hawkins claimed that I "voluntarily left last work without good cause . . ." and/or "was discharged for misconduct." Hawkins' attorney was sheepish about the whole thing and was making noises about the appeal having to be filed hastily in the wake of my "threats" to expose the firm to bad publicity. Mona told Betsy that appealing could turn out to be an expensive decision for Hawkins because, for a lousy couple hundred dollars a week, they now had another stubborn lawyer to deal with. Mona also mentioned that the appeal really undermined Hawkins' *bona fides* about the underlying "ethics reason" (not being able to trust my judgment) for their decision-making.

Three days later I got the advance copy of the *New Yorker* article. In a sprawling investigative spread, Jane, who was privy to information I did not have, was able to document the cover-up:

> An official list compiled by the prosecution confirms that the Justice Department did not hand over Radack's most critical e-mail, in which she questioned the viability

of Lindh's confession, until after her confrontation with Flynn.

Vindication, at last, from a well-respected magazine famed for its fact-checking department.

The next day I was bombarded with press inquiries from NPR, CBS News, "60 Minutes," and the *New York Times*. Conspicuously absent was the *Washington Post*. I also was called by former *New York Times* columnist Tony Lewis, Legal Director of the ACLU Steve Shapiro, Senior Minority Counsel on the House Judiciary Committee Burt Wides, and the office of Congressman Waxman, who was the Ranking Democratic Member on the House Committee on Government Reform. Rick advised me to lay low and gauge the public reaction. It could either make the case against me harder to prosecute, or make the Justice Department more determined to get me. If you hit the Justice Department too hard in public, they are locked in and need to discredit you.

Somewhere far away, white supremacists assaulted John Walker Lindh in prison.

The Defense Department's chief counsel, at the behest of Guantánamo Bay commanders, prepared a draft of a classified Pentagon report, dated March 6, 2003. The 100-plus-page report's central argument was radical: normal strictures on torture don't apply because nothing is more important than "obtaining intelligence vital to the protection of untold thousands of American citizens."

Much of the reasoning in the Pentagon report adopted the arguments of the January and August 2002 memos. The report outlined U.S. laws and international treaties forbidding torture and, using the Strangelovian logic of dictatorships and totalitarian governments around the world, argued that those restrictions could be overcome by "national security" considerations or legal technicalities. In lock-step with the original Gonzales memo, the report advised that the President wasn't bound by domestic and international laws prohibiting torture because he has the authority as Commander-in-Chief to approve almost any physical or psychological actions during interrogation, up to and including torture. Suspected terrorists could be treated like the alleged heretics hauled before the Inquisition: they were not permitted to face their accusers, they were not allowed to mount a defense, innocence was wholly irrelevant, and creative torture was the preferred method for obtaining confessions.

This perversion of the Commander-in-Chief clause regresses the Constitution 800 years to a time before the Magna Carta. It flies in the face of years of Supreme Court precedent that has repeatedly rejected expansive claims of absolute control by the Executive. In *Youngstown Sheet and Tube Co. v. Sawyer*, the Supreme Court rejected President Truman's unilateral attempt to take over private steel mills to forestall a strike during the Korean War. Justice O'Connor, tellingly, would later cite this case in one of the enemy combatant decisions, with her statement that "a state of war is not a blank check for the president when it comes to the rights of the nation's citizens." While the president has significant latitude in the conduct of foreign affairs, this leeway has been constrained by congressional legislation and judicial decisions to prevent the transmogrification of the President into an absolute monarch.

According to the newly-espoused Commander-in-Chief logic, President Bush may authorize abuse and still plausibly *claim*, as he has assured the public in the aftermath of the leaked Justice Department torture memo and Pentagon report, that he "adhere[s] to law." He testily told reporters, "That ought to comfort you." But President Bush's reassurances are not comforting because his Administration's documents argue that no law banning torture or regulating interrogation can bind the President when he is acting as Commander-in-Chief. As Harold Hongju Koh, dean of Yale Law School, pointed out, if the President has Commander-in-Chief power to commit torture, he has the power to order genocide, sanction slavery, promote apartheid, license summary execution, and commit numerous other human rights atrocities.

The Pentagon report also advised that government agents and civilian or military personnel who might torture prisoners at the President's direction couldn't be prosecuted by the Justice Department for torture or other war crimes. With astonishing premeditation, it even outlined potential legal defenses, including the "necessity" of using torture techniques to extract information to prevent an attack, and the so-called "Nuremberg defense" of following "superior orders" that render moral choice illusory. The Nuremberg defense excuses questionable practices with the legal excuse that if actions were undertaken by command, then the burden of guilt is lifted. This was the legal argument used by the Nazi war criminals on trial after World War II. The judges at Nuremberg rejected this "just following orders" defense. And the Yugoslav and Rwandan war crimes tribunals, which have been enforcing international criminal law for the past ten years, have also rejected the Nuremberg defense.

But the Bush Administration single-handedly and unilaterally redefined torture. It officially endorsed principles relied on in the past by the military *juntas* in Argentina and Chile, and by autocracies such as Algeria and Uzbekistan today, which claim that torture is justified when used to combat terrorism. Even if the Administration's theories were never put into practice, as its officials stubbornly maintain, the report's eventual revelation put an unremovable stain on Jeffersonian democracy.

When the torture memo and the Pentagon report eventually became public in June 2004, the Bush Administration refused to disclose, or even provide to Congress, copies of them, despite a fusillade of public criticism stemming from leaks to several newspapers – and an independent press that was willing to print them. These memos reveal nothing less than that the U.S. government, acting carefully and with legal counsel, deliberately sought to evade U.S. and international laws.

At home I watched the TV movie, "The Pentagon Papers." I had been a newborn baby when Defense Department whistleblower Daniel Ellsberg leaked to the press the government's secret history of the Vietnam War. The White House and Justice Department tried to "neutralize" him. "It took months. It took over my life," his character said. Nixon and Mitchell. Bush and Ashcroft. It sounded all too familiar. Bush is a more dishonest president than Richard Nixon, a conclusion supported by everyone from the predictable, like former Vice President Al Gore, to Nixon's White House counsel, John Dean. The post-Watergate reforms, which were supposed to have reined in the government in response to earlier abuses and that were intended to prevent political harassment, have been cast aside cavalierly.

Burt Wides was friends with Senator Edward Kennedy's chief counsel, Jim Flug, and suggested to Flug that Kennedy question the Justice Department about my situation. On March 11, 2003, Senator Kennedy submitted written questions to Attorney General Ashcroft following a Judiciary Committee hearing in early March on "The War Against Terrorism: Working Together to Protect America." Question #9 was a page-long series of inquiries regarding my situation as reported in *The New Yorker:*

Was Ms. Radack in fact forced
to leave her position at the Justice
Department because of the ethical

113

advice she provided on the interrogation of Mr. Lindh? Have you conducted any investigation into the withholding of e-mails from the federal court in the Lindh case? Have any employees other than Ms. Radack been disciplined? Is Ms. Radack in fact now the target of a criminal investigation by the U.S. Attorney's office? For what is she being investigated?

Senator Kennedy asked all the right questions, none of which were ever answered. From my experience, it was unlike the Justice Department to blow off Congressional correspondence, especially from someone of Kennedy's stature – the second most senior member of the Senate and one who serves on the Judiciary Committee. I drafted a couple of Congressional responses myself while at Justice and they were always given careful attention. But Ashcroft gained a reputation for treating Congress as irrelevant.

The unemployment compensation hearing initiated by Hawkins was held on St. Patrick's Day. We were all wearing green, so it made for a comical sight. Years later, I learned that on the morning of the hearing, Agent Powell of the Justice Department's OIG "met with Cullen MacDonald and [Hawkins' attorney Betsy] Plevan at the law firm of Hawkins, Delafield & Wood . . . to provide an affidavit to be presented to the Unemployment Compensation Appeals

Division" – something Americans of any political stripe should find outrageous. Since when does the government orchestrate the firing of a private citizen from a private firm, and then assist the private firm in its quest to terminate the employee's receipt of unemployment benefits? The Justice Department's enlistment of a private firm to act as its agent in retaliating against a former employee should offend the sensibilities of even the most right-wing Republican.

The hearing lasted over three hours and was all over the map. Mona represented me brilliantly at the hearing and was able to get Hawkins to admit that my "misconduct" was nothing more than the exercise of my constitutional right not to cooperate with a government investigation wholly unrelated to my current employment. Hawkins' position was reminiscent of the campaign aimed at suspected Communists led by Senator Joseph McCarthy and the House Un-American Activities Committee. Targets of the committee were confronted with information from informers, but had no opportunity to cross-examine their accusers and no access to evidence in the possession of the government that would assist their defense. Those who refused to testify by invoking the Fifth Amendment often lost their jobs and were ostracized from their communities.

MacDonald was a surly leprechaun throughout the proceeding. He accused me of "defrauding" the firm and threatened to sue me for getting myself hired under "false pretenses" because I did not tell Hawkins about the Lindh quagmire. (In point of fact, I had told Hawkins when interviewing that I wanted to leave the ethics office because I felt it was not behaving very ethically.) He also told me in a "Gotcha!" tone of voice that the firm had turned over my computer to the government. Never mind that there was no warrant for it. In an all-too-common over-reading of the Patriot Act, such things were being done throughout our country. Never mind that, in turning over my computer, Hawkins willingly gave the government loads of attorney-client privileged communications about its other clients. Talk about a massive breach of privilege! But I'll leave it to Hawkins' clients to be outraged at the firm for so willingly giving Uncle Sam privileged communications regarding their private legal matters, which were entirely unrelated to the investigation of me. Finally, MacDonald said menacingly that something "huge" was going to happen. Obviously, the government was still making him big promises.

On March 19th, we went to war with Iraq. The film *Wag the Dog*, about a president who fabricated a war to deflect his own failures, had become eerily prophetic. Two days later, Baghdad was flattened in a day described only and repeatedly as "shock and awe." It was a televised event. The propaganda machine was in overdrive. It was like watching a video game – the viewer was engrossed in it and removed at the same time. It was "all Iraq, all the time" on every major television network.

We learned from Hawkins that Agent Powell had done a declaration, which *could* indicate that there was some sort of grand jury activity going on. For what? Theft of government property for taking copies of my e-mails, which would not have existed had I not resurrected them from the computer archives? At the U.S. Attorney's Office, Nash said he'd talk to Rick before "doing anything," but that didn't increase my comfort level. Rick and Mona detected that Hawkins' mood to negotiate seemed to lessen – they were emboldened by something. MacDonald's "warning" that something big was coming down the pike echoed in my ears. We strategized with Burt Wides about how to let Justice know that Congress was watching, without pushing so hard that the Department would file charges in order to sully my name.

On a bright note, I won the appeal of my unemployment compensation benefits. The hearing officer wrote a great opinion, which rejected the firm's claim that my refusing to talk to the IG was "misconduct" that justified termination of my employment.

Three days later, on March 27th, the Justice Department issued an agency-wide gag order in response to a request by Ashcroft. It mandated that employees had to clear any contacts with Congress through Justice's Congressional liaison office. This order was in direct contradiction of the First Amendment, the Lloyd-LaFollette Act, and the Whistleblower Protection Act. In what was news to me, I learned that Justice had an interagency anti-leak task force, which recommended that government administrators punish employees who leak information. It made me think of the "Alien Border Control Committee," another Justice Department interagency task force organized in 1986 to develop plans for the deportation of alien activists critical of U.S. policies if they were "not in conformity with their immigration status." It foreshadowed the post-September 11th use of immigration laws to disrupt political activities of people who were not engaged in criminal conduct, but who happened to be of the "wrong" religion or nationality. Too bad the anti-leak task force's objectives weren't applied to the "two senior administration officials" from the White House who leaked information that destroyed the career of former ambassador Joseph Wilson's wife, or that destroyed the career of Steven Hatfill, or that derailed my career.

A reporter from the *National Law Journal* called Rick and said he thought I was a "hero." But I didn't feel so heroic those days. I was on pins and needles waiting for a mystery indictment to come down.

11. Senator Kennedy and "This Radack Situation"

My law school mentor put me back in touch with a classmate, Robin Toone, who was now counsel for Senator Kennedy on the Senate Judiciary Committee.

The Pentagon Working Group completed the review it had commenced in mid-January and issued an 85-page report dated April 4, 2003. It reviewed "legal, historical, policy and operational considerations," and made recommendations to the Pentagon on what techniques should be approved. It adopted the arguments of Bybee's August 2002 memo, noting that, "Due to the unique nature of the war on terrorism . . . the interrogation of unlawful combatants in a manner beyond that which may be applied to a prisoner of war" may be necessary. The next paragraph warns that "[s]hould information regarding the use of more aggressive interrogation techniques . . . become public, it is likely to be exaggerated or distorted in the U.S. and international media accounts, and may produce an adverse effect on support for the war on terrorism."

The Judge Advocates General for the Army, Air Force and Marines expressed their concerns as the policy was being hashed out at the Pentagon in March and April, worrying that harsh interrogation tactics would not only cause public outrage if they ever came to light, but would also contravene long-standing military doctrine.

Four days later, I got an e-mail from a Hawkins colleague and confidant, Jill Cork, informing me that the office manager was going to pack up everything in my office. No one had told me I was fired; in fact, three weeks earlier Hawkins argued in the unemployment hearing that I still worked there.

Mona said it was nothing more than Hawkins continuing to act uncivilized. She asked Hawkins if this indirect chatter meant that I had been fired, and suggested that Hawkins stop being so circumspect about its adverse employment actions. Hawkins asked what we should do about the entire situation, and Mona said I wasn't going to resign because that would cut off my claim to back pay in the lawsuit we were going to bring against them. Hawkins' lawyer asked if Mona had any other ideas about how to terminate my employment without compromising anyone's rights. Mona suggested that Hawkins call a spade a spade, and stop shrugging its shoulders about what my status was: fired. Hawkins then said they didn't want to fire me because that could prejudice them down the road. It was a standoff. By that point, if I still truly "worked" there, the firm owed me five months of back pay. But they really wanted to have it both ways – not to fire me "because it might prejudice them down the road," and not to pay me or let me return to work because it would displease the government.

We weren't to the point of a wrongful termination lawsuit yet. We needed to end the threat of criminal prosecution, which was leaving me hamstrung in terms of a civil action against Justice or Hawkins.

Meanwhile, Rick spoke with Nash in the U.S. Attorney's Office, who was angry about the quote attributed to him in *The New Yorker* about my case being "on the back burner." They were, Nash insisted, very interested in it. I thought, so why don't they *do* something? Anything. And so what if the quote made the government look ambivalent? The article still got across the point that I was most ashamed of: there was an active criminal investigation of me. I felt as if I had been placed in legal purgatory with the likes of Steven Hatfill and Wen Ho Lee, or more recently Captain James Yee, where the government had decided I'd done something wrong and was bound and determined to get me. The Army arrested Yee – an American citizen, West Point graduate, Muslim convert, and chaplain at the Guantánamo Bay prison – leaked his arrest to the press, smeared him with inflammatory potential charges (sedition, aiding the enemy, spying, espionage, and failure to obey a general order), threw him in solitary confinement for 76 days, subjected him to prohibited sleep- and sensory-deprivation techniques, and humiliated him at a pre-court-martial hearing before dropping all charges against him and putting him back on active duty as if nothing had ever happened (except, of course, slapping a gag order on him so that he couldn't talk about the mistreatment).

Curiously, Nash asked who was paying my legal fees, a wholly inappropriate question because such information is privileged. Rick suspected that if it had been Judicial Watch or *Newsweek*, Justice would have been more likely to go after me. That really opened my eyes to how politicized the whole thing was and how it had nothing to do with the merits of what really happened. After I waived the privilege, Rick told Nash that I was paying out of my own pocket, but that we might have to consider getting bankrolled by someone else at some point because it was getting expensive and I had lost my job. Nash said he was well aware of my employment situation.

Of course he was. The Justice Department had orchestrated it.

Rick suggested to Nash that someone at Justice ought to focus on the substance of what was in *The New Yorker*. Apparently, a lot of people at the Department were doing just that – but their goal was to shut me up, not find out what really happened.

Rumsfeld, acting on the Pentagon Working Groups' recommendation, reissued his guidance for Guantánamo Bay on April 16, 2003. He sent General Hill a memo approving 24 interrogation techniques, four of which were considered harsh enough to require Rumsfeld's explicit approval. The removal of clothing, while earlier approved by Rumsfeld for use at Guantánamo Bay, was not among the authorized techniques in his revised guidelines, but at least five of the other modified high-pressure techniques were later listed in an October 9th Abu Ghraib memo.

As the major combat ended in Iraq (or so we were led to believe), I served on federal jury duty from April 16th to the 22nd. No one questioned my patriotism for that onerous civic duty. I'm only unpatriotic when it suits the government's interests.

Another law review article of mine was accepted by the *William & Mary Bill of Rights Journal*, this one entitled "United States Citizens Detained as 'Enemy Combatants': The Right to Counsel as a Matter of Ethics." The personal continued to be political. I was writing like a maniac on matters close to my heart. I wasn't writing about my own personal experience, but rather about enemy combatants and government whistleblowers as a purely academic matter. It was safe that way. It was a cathartic outlet in the highbrow genre of legal academia and it strengthened my reputation as an expert in legal ethics.

I was invited to teach a session of Owen Fiss' "Metaprocedure" class at Yale Law School, which was uplifting. I got a warm reception. Professor Fiss, whom I never had as a teacher, was very complimentary and gave me a great and flattering introduction. He had read my enemy combatant paper with resounding approval. I felt as if I had intelligent things to say during the Q and A and really had developed an expertise to share with the students. "We take care of our own," one of the deans reminded me.

The following week I gave a speech before the Philadelphia Bar Association, which honored me "for her conduct as a lawyer, at the great expense to her personal career. Not only should she be honored for behaving at the highest professional standards, but our commending her in a public way may call attention to the very highhanded and unfair predicament in which she now finds herself." My speech was well received. I was preaching to the choir, but it still meant a lot to me.

NBC World News Tonight featured an FBI whistleblower, Jane Turner, who reported the theft of a globe from Ground Zero. She received a scathing performance evaluation, which sounded a lot like mine. They were shooting the messenger, rather than addressing the message by investigating the underlying misconduct about which she complained.

The Justice Department, to which the FBI reports, gained quite a reputation for its retaliation against whistleblowers. After John Roberts, a unit chief in the FBI's Office of Professional Responsibility, discussed FBI shortcomings with "60 Minutes," his supervisor disciplined him. After FBI translator Sibel Edmonds complained to her supervisor about poor management, slow progress, incompetence and corruption, she was fired. The Justice Department invoked the rarely used "state secrets privilege" to prevent her from providing evidence, and retroactively classified testimony by FBI officials that corroborated her story. The agency also retaliated against former FBI agent Mike German, an undercover specialist who once infiltrated a white supremacist group of skinheads, for complaining about a botched anti-terrorism investigation.

My case was stagnant. It appeared that it was, in fact, "on the back burner." To the extent the Justice Department was a sleeping dog, did we want to disturb it? We had already prodded it once with *The New Yorker* article. But as Dan pointed out, the problem with letting sleeping dogs lie is that this dog was lying on top of me.

The decision about whether to grant requests for press interviews was soon made for me during a surreal month from May to June during which I became embroiled in the confirmation hearing of Michael Chertoff, the Assistant Attorney General of the Justice Department's Criminal Division, who was nominated to be a judge on the Third Circuit Court of Appeals. He was considered a relatively vanilla Republican compared to far more objectionable judicial nominees like Janice Rogers Brown, Pricilla Owen, Charles Pickering, William Pryor and Carolyn Kuhl.

Chertoff was forty-nine years old. He was gaunt and balding with a thin, stubbly beard. His intellectual prowess made him the inspiration for an intense and brilliant character in his Harvard Law School classmate Scott Turow's bestselling book, *One L*, about their days as first-year law students. He made his name prosecuting Fat Tony Salerno, the mobster and a former Genovese family boss, and Crazy Eddie, the once ubiquitous electronics retailer, who referred to him as "Count Chertoff." Others referred to him using the unflattering synonym for masturbation that rhymed with his name.

In a more embarrassing chapter of Chertoff's otherwise meteoric career, he had worked as special counsel to the Senate committee that investigated the Whitewater affair. He gave serious consideration to wild Clinton conspiracy theories and belabored Vincent Foster's suicide. He had previously cultivated an apolitical reputation, but Whitewater marked his emergence as a staunch Republican, which ultimately won him an important future patron in then-Senator Ashcroft.

His office at the Justice Department had now become the epicenter of the most important criminal investigation in American history: September 11th. He had been the senior Justice official on duty at the FBI command center when the terrorist attacks occurred.

On May 7, 2003, my law school classmate, Robin Toone, informed me that Senator Kennedy asked Chertoff about the Lindh interrogation during Chertoff's nomination hearing.

Chertoff, incredibly, denied that PRAO ever took a position on the Lindh interrogation, despite the fact that the public record contradicted his denial.

"I have to say, Senator, I think that the Professional Responsibility [Advisory] Office was not asked for advice in this matter. I was involved in it."

He couldn't stop the embellishment. "Mr. Lindh was Mirandized, and had he requested counsel or requested to invoke his right to silence at the point at which the FBI was involved, they would have honored that request." This second part was, at best, a gross mischaracterization of what happened and at worst, perjury. As Jane Mayer's uncontroverted article documented, "[FBI Agent] Reimann read Lindh the Miranda warning. But, when noting the right to counsel, the agent now acknowledges, he ad-libbed, 'Of course there are no lawyers here.'"

Senator Kennedy asked Chertoff a second time, "[D]o you remember what the Professional Responsibility Advisory Office['s] . . . position was on this?"

"I was not consulted with respect to this matter," Chertoff answered. "There are other parts of the Department that generally render opinions in this area of the law and other expertise that was consulted."

Kennedy persevered. "Well, your statement that the Professional Responsibility Advisory Office did not have an official position on this —"

"I don't believe they had an official position on this," Chertoff interrupted.

It seemed so odd to me that Chertoff would deny that the ethics office ever took a position on the Lindh matter in light of stories to the contrary that had appeared in *Newsweek* and *The New Yorker*. It was clear to me that he was trying to protect Claudia. They had both worked together in the U.S. Attorney's Office for the District of New Jersey.

I suggested to Robin that Kennedy question Chertoff about whether Chertoff was part of the decision to conceal Judge Ellis' discovery order from me. I also suggested that Kennedy might want to ask whether or not Claudia Flynn was ever investigated for not telling me, an attorney under her direct supervision, that there was a federal court order that covered my e-mail. Heck, why not ask Chertoff whether he was concerned that the *ethics* office had been accused of behaving in a way that was entirely unethical, including destroying evidence and obstructing justice? I was seething that Chertoff was going to effortlessly lie his way into a federal judgeship.

I met with Eric Lichtblau of the *New York Times* and Douglas McCollam of *The American Lawyer*, followed by a Mother's Day tea at Jacob's school. They served us drinks and cake and sang a sweet song:

> Inch by inch, row by row,
> We're gonna make this garden grow
> All it takes is a rake and a hoe
> And a piece of *fertile ground*.

> Inch by inch, row by row
> Someone bless these *seeds* I sow
> Someone warm them from below
> Till the rain comes tumblin' down.

Two days later I learned I was pregnant.

Meanwhile, Senator Kennedy submitted written follow-up questions to Chertoff. I was incredulous that, this time around, Chertoff lied in *writing*, and that he didn't seize the opportunity to massage, clarify, or revise his earlier answers.

The written questions asked how the e-mails in *Newsweek* were consistent with Chertoff's testimony that PRAO never took a position on Lindh's interrogation.

Chertoff repeated, again, that,

> [T]hose at the Department responsible for the Lindh matter before and during the time of Lindh's interrogations did not to my knowledge seek PRAO's advice. I am not aware that PRAO ever took an official position about the Lindh interrogation or that any views expressed by an individual PRAO attorney were documented, factually and legally substantiated, reviewed and authorized, as I would expect before an official opinion was rendered. The e-mail traffic that you cite appears to be the impressions of a single PRAO attorney, without factual analysis and case law discussion, and therefore would not constitute an official opinion.

Years later, when I obtained a copy of the OIG leak report, it revealed that De Pue's superiors were upset that he had sought PRAO's advice about Lindh's questioning. A supervisor "informed me that the criminal division's leadership was disturbed that I had sought PRAO's advice in this matter," De Pue said in his statement to the OIG. Eric Lichtblau of the *New York Times* got De Pue to go on the record that "[t]he front office was unhappy with the fact that I had gone to PRAO with my inquiry. I was more or less told that I was out of line in making that inquiry. It was not a popular thing to do, but I thought at the time it was the reasonable thing to do . . ." According to the article, De Pue understood that the displeasure was coming from Chertoff.

Chertoff also began to lay the groundwork for dismissing PRAO's advice. He denied knowledge that PRAO's advice was sought, but then, apparently as a fallback position, preemptively discounted any advice that came from a "single individual," saying it would not be "an official position" that comports with his understanding of how "an official opinion" is rendered. He dismissed the e-mail traffic as merely a lone attorney's unsolicited, legally inadequate, fanciful musings.

I knew it would come to this: a personal attack. And this was only the tip of the iceberg. However, no amount of bracing for a punch can ever really prepare you for the hit.

Senator Kennedy next asked about my being extorted out of my job with the bogus performance evaluation, about the e-mails being withheld from the Court, and about Justice notifying the managing partner of my law firm that I was the target of a "criminal investigation." Chertoff conveniently denied having any knowledge about my employment, performance or departure.

"Has any investigation been conducted into the alleged withholding of e-mails from the federal court in the Lindh case?" Kennedy then asked, "Was Claudia J. Flynn, Director of PRAO, investigated in relation to these events? Have any Justice Department employees other than

Ms. Radack been reprimanded or disciplined in any way?"

"It would be improper for me to comment on whether Ms. Flynn was investigated," Chertoff responded. He cited a provision of the U.S. Attorney's Manual in support of his refusal.

"Is Ms. Radack the target of a criminal investigation by the U.S. Attorney's Office? For what is she being investigated?" Kennedy followed up.

Chertoff again cited a provision of the U.S. Attorney's Manual and said that it would be improper for him to comment on whether I was under investigation and, if so, about what my status might be. I found this especially hypocritical because, while Chertoff claimed with a straight face that it would be improper for him to tell the Senate Judiciary Committee whether I was under investigation, the Department of Justice felt perfectly comfortable sharing this sensitive information with my private law firm.

Chertoff's nomination was held over for another week because Kennedy wanted to submit even more questions.

This time, Chertoff finally came clean. Kennedy tried to nail him down on when and how he became aware of the contact between John De Pue and me.

Chertoff disavowed knowledge that, at the time PRAO was contacted, he *knew* PRAO was being contacted, or knew of the advice we rendered. He did finally admit, however, that he "first became aware of contacts on this issue between anyone in the Criminal Division and

PRAO after Lindh waived his Miranda rights (including his right to counsel) and consented to his December 9 and 10 interviews."

Chertoff now magically "recalled" – though he did not say what sparked his recovered memory – that the e-mail traffic "came to my attention as an outgrowth of the prosecutors' review of documents in connection with the Lindh case."

Kennedy next tried to nail down Chertoff's contention that PRAO's advice somehow would not constitute an "official opinion" because it "appears to be the impressions of a single PRAO attorney without factual analysis and case law discussion." Kennedy pointed out how the e-mail states that I consulted with a senior legal advisor. He also pointed out how the e-mail contains the qualifier that, "This opinion is based on the facts as presented and described above and in our telephone conversation."

In a non-responsive response, Chertoff claimed that he did not know with whom I consulted or what other facts were discussed in my telephone conversations.

Kennedy also zeroed in on Chertoff's artificial distinction between "unofficial" and "official" opinions:

> Isn't it customary for PRAO attorneys to provide opinions on professional responsibility matters via e-mail; to base their opinions on the facts presented to them by other Justice Department employees; and not to cite case law unless

specifically asked to[,] particularly when the applicable legal authority is already set forth in existing PRAO memoranda [that are available Department-wide] . . . and when the inquiry is time-sensitive? Are there any Justice Department policies or regulations that distinguish between 'unofficial' and 'official' PRAO opinions, or are you applying your own subjective standard on this issue?

Chertoff's answer was obtuse. He conveniently disavowed knowledge of PRAO's customary practice in rendering advice, but admitted that his earlier comments were based on his own "personal beliefs," "expectations," and subjective standards. Yet in a Bush-like demonstration of stubbornness and arrogance, he claimed that he still didn't know whether PRAO had taken an "official position" on the issue of Lindh's interrogation. He then offered his unsolicited "personal opinion" that, as a legal matter, the interrogation was proper. As an ethics matter, however, in an amazing exhibit of his moral blind spot, Chertoff cited, in support of his opinion, the old federal regulation that was superseded by the McDade law from which PRAO had been created. He also dismissed the opinion as two attorneys merely "exchanging their views." Finally, he stated erroneously that because a law enforcement agent, not a lawyer, had interrogated Lindh, then no attorney could be implicated.

This faulty reasoning emerged again in the Abu Ghraib scandal, and again in Chertoff's confirmation hearing to be head of Homeland Security. The ethics rules governing attorneys state that a lawyer should be held responsible for the conduct and activities of agents or investigators acting on the lawyer's behalf or who are associated with the lawyer. No wonder Rumsfeld wanted to cut lawyers out of the picture. He mocked lawyers as worrywart bureaucrats and nit-pickers, and resented the "legalistic hurdles" that got in the way of doing what he wanted. "Reduce the number of lawyers," he said. "They are like beavers – they get in the middle of the stream and dam it up."

As it turns out, I wasn't the only one who raised concerns about Chertoff's behavior. Judicial Watch, a private government watchdog group, made accusations that the FBI improperly used organized crime figures as informants in the District of New Jersey while Chertoff was the U.S. Attorney there during the early 1990s. Lichtblau's article in the *New York Times* came out and the headline read "Dispute Over Legal Advice Costs a Job and Complicates a Nomination." Kennedy was quoted in the article as saying, "I'm very concerned about this Radack situation." My husband, a Massachusetts native, cut out the quote, enlarged it, and put it up at work.

The controversy culminated in a contentious Senate Judiciary hearing in which the Committee voted 13-0, with all six Democrats effectively abstaining, to send

Chertoff's nomination to the full Senate for consideration.

Democrats requested a second delay in the vote on Chertoff, which angered Hatch, who attacked Lichtblau for his article and the delay it had caused in voting on Chertoff. Hatch claimed that the article was an unfair effort to "smear this acclaimed public servant," Chertoff.

"It's disgraceful at this last minute the *New York Times* is attempting to impugn anybody," Hatch said. "Lichtblau shared bylines with the infamous Mr. Blair," the *Times* reporter who had recently resigned for fabricating stories. Talk about unfairly impugning someone.

Leahy then accused Hatch of McCarthyism for making such a low blow against Lichtblau. Hatch agreed to conduct a bipartisan investigation into Judicial Watch's allegations about misuse of federal informants.

Senator Kennedy, in a moving and strongly-worded public statement on the nomination, expressed his dissatisfaction with Chertoff's elliptical answers:

> Last week I expressed my concern about Mr. Chertoff's failure to provide serious, consistent, and responsive answers to the questions asked by members of this Committee. In particular, his answers to my first set of written questions were non-responsive, evasive, and hyper-technical. They were stingy in substance, avoiding the questions that were asked, and

often answering questions that were not asked. . . . At last week's Committee meeting, I asked my good friend, the Chairman, to hold Mr. Chertoff's nomination over for another week. . . . Evasive and non-responsive answers will not do – no matter how 'uncontroversial' a nomination may otherwise be.

Though it received little play in the press, Kennedy's statement about Chertoff's misleading answers said it better than I ever could. Even though Kennedy ultimately supported Chertoff's nomination, as I knew all along that he would, it was still extremely validating to have Chertoff called out on the carpet.

On June 9, 2003, Chertoff was confirmed. All voted in favor except Senator Clinton.

Chertoff has supposedly resisted commenting on what happened in my case because, he has "to be careful to not get into matters that are not public." This defense is betrayed by the fact that the Department of Justice has regularly shared non-public information with my private law firm, the media, and the state bars in which I am licensed to practice law. As Michael Tigar, one of the nation's top defense lawyers, has pointed out, "Under the Bush/Ashcroft/Rumsfeld Administration, the independent press and the independent bar have been in particular danger . . . This Administration has tried to intimidate, manipulate, harass, and if necessary punish any independent voice that questions its relentless pursuit of power." Tigar represented Lynne Stewart, whose case drew the attention of defense lawyers across the country who saw it as an attempt by the government to scare them away from representing unpopular clients.

It galled me that Chertoff would now sit in judgment of others and make $167,000 a year for doing it. I only hoped that those who appeared before him would take their oath to tell the truth more seriously than Chertoff took his. He perjured himself at my expense – an accusation I don't make lightly – in order to get a promotion, lifetime tenure, and the prestige of being a federal judge.

12. The Sword of Damocles

I started to receive warnings from a number of reporters that one of my former colleagues at PRAO, Joan Goldfrank, was reaching out to them and trashing me. Joan became the self-appointed attack dog, taking it upon herself to contact reporters whenever she learned there was an article on my situation in the works. It appears that whenever Claudia was called for comment, she would immediately pick up the phone and tip off Joan, the unofficial opposition spokesperson.

Joan told reporters that my husband basically "left me" for long periods on travel and I was essentially a "single mother." She said I wrote men's names on a so-called "Rape List" at Brown University. She even went so far as to say that *I* was the obstructer in the Lindh case – that I removed the e-mails from the PRAO file – a ridiculous accusation that would require an impossible degree of premeditation and orchestration. What earthly reason would I have to remove the e-mails, unhesitatingly highlight such a dastardly act on my part, go to such excruciating lengths to resurrect the e-mails, and throw away my career to expose them? Joan didn't realize the significance of her accusation: it was the first time anyone who had been at PRAO *admitted* that the e-mails were missing from the file. The Justice Department had never denied this fact, but it had never acknowledged it either. Instead, Justice's position seemed to be that since at least some of the e-mails eventually reached the court (we'll never know for sure how many because the Justice Department has strenuously resisted unsealing the "documents" they claim to be my e-mail), then no harm, no foul.

Joan's behavior was actually classic treatment of whistleblowers: smears of purported misconduct similar to what the employee was alleging. In my case, the smear included accusing me of unethical conduct – purging the file when *they* in fact had done the purging, and breaching attorney-client privilege when they were the ones who had abused it and committed illegal acts under its cover. Joan failed to realize that digging up dirt on your accuser is widely viewed not as part of your defense, but as indicative that you have none.

I think part of Joan's strategy was to sling mud at me just to hear me deny it. Lyndon Johnson once told a top aide, Joe Califano, to leak to a friendly reporter that Senator John McClellan was holding up a budget bill because he wanted the government to build a dam on the land he owned. When Califano asked whether that was true, LBJ told the tale of an old Texas congressman who once falsely accused an opponent of sleeping with sheep, just to make the man deny it. Joan started all sorts of ugly rumors, just to make me have to deny them. We eventually had to send her a "cease and desist" letter because her defamation had reached such extraordinary heights.

Laurie Abraham, an acquaintance from Yale Law School, started writing an article for

139

the *New York Times Magazine.* I thought this was a good thing because it was a reputable medium and a magazine article could provide more texture than newspaper articles.

Meanwhile, Gregg Leslie of The Reporters' Committee for Freedom of the Press buttonholed Isikoff at a journalists' conference and asked him if he was concerned about how I was being treated. According to Leslie, Iskioff was not concerned. Iskioff said that the Department of Justice was just trying to scare me. As if that were okay. As if *that*, in itself, were not a story.

The American Lawyer ran an article in July. It was positive, but I thought Hawkins got off scot-free. As of the summer of 2003, Hawkins still had me listed as an Associate on Martindale Hubbell (a database of over one million lawyers and law firms in 160 countries), kept my voice mail activated, and called me at home to give me personal messages. They wouldn't pay me and wouldn't allow me to come to work, yet they told *The American Lawyer* that I was still employed by them – just on something akin to "medical leave." They neglected to mention that medical leave, unlike the black hole I was in, was voluntary, often entailed some kind of compensation, and guaranteed you a place when you returned. Imperfect analogies aside, Hawkins wouldn't admit the truth: the government was leaning on them to get rid of me and they didn't want to get on the wrong side of this bully Administration.

The *American Lawyer* reporter, Douglas McCollam, discovered that all the calls the government traced were from Isikoff to me, which prompted Isikoff to worry that his phone was being tapped. Isikoff wanted to see the "evidence" that Hawkins presented to us, courtesy of the U.S. government. I grudgingly obliged, though I certainly didn't feel I owed him any favors.

The media is a strange animal. The fourth estate can bring transparency to government agencies, shape public opinion, and play the role of a leveler. News reports can take disputes out of the stifling air of agency offices and into the glare of public scrutiny. Media coverage can transform a workplace "troublemaker" into a public hero and reduce an office director to a beleaguered figure whose resignation is demanded.

But the media can also try to make a story of the whistleblower. (In Laurie Abraham's eventual story, I was described as a "moral narcissist" by an "expert" who'd never met me.) Media exposure can additionally inflame the agency against you as it finds itself on the defensive in an embarrassing public forum. And a story's effects can be evanescent. The public attention span is surprisingly short. New distractions manufactured by the person on whom you're blowing the whistle can steal the public's attention. The Bush Administration is especially adept at this bait-and-switch routine.

Most laypersons are not schooled in knowing a reporter's "beat," creating a "hook" for the story without having it buried in their own back, laying "ground rules," going "off the record," or speaking "on background." I believe journalists have a duty to educate sources at

141

least minimally. Isikoff didn't; in fact, he asked if I wanted to be quoted in the article.

"Won't that identify me as the source?" I asked.

"Yeah, probably," he said. He should have volunteered this near-certainty. He didn't let me know that the information alone would reveal me as the probable source, that the e-mails would be published in full on the magazine's website, or that I should not take his calls at work (and he should not have called me at work).

I have turned down the majority of media requests, and only agreed to print media over which we had more control, not broadcast media such as TV or radio. Anytime someone did an article, it caused me tremendous "publication anxiety." It stressed me out to continually have to clarify, rebut and confirm what other people said. It was exhausting.

I have a cautious relationship with reporters. Some have done unspeakable good – Jane Mayer, Eric Lichtblau, Gregg Leslie, Douglas McCollam, Emily Gold Boutilier – and others have hurt me, and hurt the public's right to know what their government was doing, even if unintentionally. There is an unavoidable tendency for reporters to want to "try the case" in the media. And it is hard to shine the spotlight on the issue and not on yourself. People usually leak anonymously, as I did, so the media will focus on the message without exposing the messenger. But can the media really deliver the message, and not the messenger? Reporters like to add drama to their stories and the tortured whistleblower angle is ripe for exploitation. Additionally, every article enraged the political appointees at the Justice Department and always provoked some sort of retaliatory response. It was like waking the sleeping giant. Media coverage never had the surefire "bullet proofing" effect of deterring Justice from attacking me.

Strange bedfellows have been a recurring phenomenon throughout my saga, so it was serendipitous but not shocking that Bruce Fein came into my life, just like one of those deeply-appreciated surprises when Jane Mayer showed up on my doorstep or when Senator Kennedy took up my cause. My uncle, Al Guttman, is a real estate lawyer who rents office space to other lawyers. One of his tenants is the legendary constitutional law expert Bruce Fein, and my uncle kept urging me to meet him. Fein's reputation preceded him. A top-level Justice Department official in the Reagan Administration, he was known for his ardent conservative credentials, so I really did not think he would take an interest in my case, which seemed so ideologically driven.

My uncle arranged a lunch for the three of us in July. Bruce is brilliant in the way that one or two people in my classes at Brown University and Yale Law School were: not just book-smart, but truly dazzling. He's lanky, pale, boyish, and unimposing. I think I weigh more than Bruce even when I'm not pregnant. He possesses an encyclopedic knowledge of history, a mastery of the classics, and has a Rolodex deeper than the Pacific Ocean, but he is not a fact-spouter or a name-dropper. He is so smart that he exhibits none of the usual insecurities that plague people who are smart, but who know that they are not true intellectuals, much less geniuses. He was also very open and I learned about his three children – his son and namesake who is an attorney serving in Baghdad, his other son who is a nationally-ranked figure skater, and his dear daughter, Hillary, who died suddenly a few years ago of a brain aneurysm. I was struck and moved by his openness and compassion, emotional traits often lacking in people so cerebral.

We ate at the Army & Navy Club and spoke easily for hours. He was familiar with my case and said he wanted to represent me. He favored taking a more aggressive approach in bringing this whole debacle to a close, for example, by seeking a letter clearing me. I was not optimistic because, as a Justice attorney, I knew first-hand that government investigations were notorious for dragging on for years and that they rarely did you the courtesy of letting you know when the case was closed. A letter actually clearing you was virtually unheard of. Bruce believed the only person ever to have received such a letter was Clark Clifford, the key advisor to four Presidents who was indicted on the basis of a Manhattan D.A.'s speculative and novel theory that two separate legal transactions somehow constituted a conspiracy of fraud and bribery.

Bruce differed with Rick Robinson's "lay low" approach and was more inclined to go on the offensive and to use the media. In the words

144

of Supreme Court Justice Louis Brandeis' elegant axiom, "Sunlight is the best disinfectant," and illumination has proven to be a cure for this secretive Administration's skewering of those who speak the truth. I told Bruce I'd have to run it by Rick, with whom Bruce was totally willing to coordinate and cooperate. My main concerns were 1) offending Rick because I had discussed my case with another lawyer (which was not my intention in meeting Bruce) and 2) incurring even more legal bills, which was enough, in and of itself, to make me nearly reject the idea out of hand.

Luckily, Rick and Bruce both behaved like dignified adults rather than territorial egomaniacs. Rick was not angry that I'd met with Bruce Fein and said he was not averse to working with him. At the end of July they had lunch and decided that Bruce would co-represent me. Moreover, Bruce was willing to do so *pro bono*, meaning free of charge! This was fantastic news, and a definite new height on my emotional roller coaster.

Bruce is a pure libertarian. Ashcroft used to be aligned with the civil libertarian wing of the conservative movement – those who opposed expanding the federal government. In a 1997 op-ed piece, Ashcroft criticized government attempts to monitor the Internet to combat crime: "We do not provide the government with phone jacks outside our homes for unlimited wiretaps. Why, then, should we grant government the Orwellian capability to listen at will and in real time to our communications across the Web?" He supported a bill that would

145

have made it more difficult for federal law enforcement to spy on citizens. His own words are the best demonstration of the hypocrisy (never mind the illegality) of the domestic warrantless wiretapping program that Eric Lichtblau and a colleague later revealed.

After September 11th, Ashcroft acted more authoritarian than libertarian. Once a critic of expanding federal law enforcement power, he now argued that the Administration could be "trusted" to wield such power with no questions asked. Ashcroft was no longer against big government. He just had his own vision of what it should look like. Conservatives who were once identified with protecting individual rights against the unchecked power of the government now claimed that the Commander in Chief was above the law and that the ends justified the means.

Bruce fervently believed that what happened to me hindered the free flow of information about government operations both within the government and to the public. "The Justice Department is going to end up like the Politburo," he was fond of saying, "with underlings telling superiors only what they want to hear."

The government is hiding what is occurring behind closed doors in what are supposed to be *public* agencies. As Elaine Scarry has observed, the Patriot Act inverts the usual public-private paradigm. It used to be that people's lives were private and the work of the government was public, but the Patriot Act creates a set of conditions that make our inner lives transparent and the workings of the government opaque. A fundamental precept of our system is that the business of "the people" should be conducted so that the citizenry can learn what is being done in their name. Instead, this Administration closes court proceedings, addictively over-classifies, hermetically seals records and issues gag orders about the way agencies conduct the public's business. And truth-tellers who shine light on government corruption are punished unmercifully in a very public way.

Bruce was determined to remove the "Sword of Damocles" that was dangling over my head. The allusion comes from the myth of Dionysius, the fourth century B.C. tyrant of Syracuse. To all appearances, he was very rich and comfortable, enjoying all the luxuries money and power could buy. He even had court flatterers to inflate his ego. One of these court flatterers was Damocles. Damocles used to make gratuitous comments to the king about his wealth and luxurious life. One day when Damocles complimented the tyrant on his abundance and power, Dionysius turned to Damocles and asked, "If you think I'm so lucky, how would you like to try out my life?"

Damocles readily agreed, and so Dionysius invited him to a banquet at which he got to sit at Dionysius' throne. Damocles was enjoying himself immensely until he noticed a sharp sword above his head, which was suspended from the ceiling by a single horsehair. This, Dionysius explained to

Damocles, was what the insecure life of a ruler was really like.

Damocles was alarmed and quickly revised his idea of what made for a good life. He asked to be excused and then eagerly returned to his poorer but safer existence.

The analogy was apt. The Department's investigation was indeed a sword hanging over my head.

Bruce drafted a "Motion to Inspect and Copy" the secret leak report that was being used to tarnish me, but to which I had no access. It was my first chance to tell my side of the story, exactly my way. Judge Ellis would finally hear my version of events and would have to confront the government's abuse of both his February discovery order and his June order calling for a three-week investigation into a certain class of people to which I did not belong. It all would be documented in a public court filing for the world to see. Forget Claudia Flynn and Joan Goldfrank. Who was I protecting? What did I have left to lose? I named names and spelled out in vivid detail who did what and when they did it. It was empowering and liberating, whether the motion was granted or not.

A D.C. law firm, with whom Laurie Abraham put me in contact, began courting me aggressively to take a new position. A partner there said they didn't give a damn about the government's investigation of me, were willing to let me work my own hours, and were defending people similarly-situated to me. It sounded like the perfect job opportunity. They asked me to come up with my ideal job schedule.

During this time, I was also invited by the ABA Task Force on Treatment of Enemy Combatants to help draft its proposal to set minimum standards for civilian defense counsel representing alleged terrorists before military commissions. At the ABA's policy-setting House of Delegates' annual meeting, the ABA passed the Military Commission Recommendation and Report overwhelmingly with no debate. I felt as if my life was getting back on track.

In late August, the Joint Staff in the Pentagon sent General Miller – who was then commander of detention operations at Guantánamo – to Iraq to assist in the startup of the Abu Ghraib prison. He was accompanied there by at least 11 senior aides from Guantánamo, including officials from the CIA and Defense Intelligence Agency. Miller brought with him Guantánamo interrogation techniques, which included forcing a Guantánamo detainee named Mohammed al-Qahtani to wear a leash, perform dog tricks, and wear women's underwear.

As the second anniversary of September 11th approached, the White House kept trying to link the September 11th attacks to Iraq, as if Saddam Hussein were somehow working with al Qaeda, a position that Bush continued to assert even after the September 11th Commission disproved it. Shortly after Miller completed his inspection of the Abu Ghraib jail, he departed Iraq on September 9th and returned to brief Pentagon officials on his ideas for using military police there to implement new high-pressure interrogation methods.

General Miller presented his interrogation rules to Lieutenant General Ricardo S. Sanchez, who was then the senior U.S. military commander in Iraq. On the eve of September 11th, Lieutenant General Sanchez personally approved an "Interrogation and Counter-Resistance Policy," which contained a series of coercive interrogation techniques, many of which went beyond the limits set in the Army's field manual and were outlawed by the Geneva Conventions.

No formalized rules for interrogation existed in Iraq before the policy imposed that day. Sanchez borrowed heavily from the infamous list of high-pressure interrogation tactics used at the detention facility in Guantánamo Bay. Sanchez approved letting senior officials at Abu Ghraib use military dogs, temperature extremes, reversed sleep patterns, sensory deprivation, and diets of bread and water on detainees whenever they wished. The 32 interrogation tactics could be imposed without first seeking the approval of anyone outside the prison, giving officers at Abu Ghraib wide latitude in handling detainees.

In May 2004, Sanchez denied under oath approving such techniques before the Senate Armed Services Committee. The ACLU obtained a copy of his memo under the Freedom of Information Act that proved he perjured himself before Congress.

Soon an actual videotape of bin Laden aired. It was chilling to see him in the flesh.

13. The Second Anniversary of 9/11

My goal on the second anniversary of September 11th, as I'm sure it was for many people, was just to make it through the day. This day represented not only the grief and loss that everyone in our country was feeling, but for me personally, a loss of the daily way of life I had known – the loss of two jobs, my privacy, friends (certain ones), solid reputation, financial security, confidence, and peace of mind. Now our country was under the "Ashcroft Doctrine," the new rules, "Bush justice," and the very undemocratic Patriot Act.

I muddled through the day, spending a lot of time remembering, thinking, reflecting and mourning. Someone we knew from this area, by the name of Linda C. Lee, had died in the Trade Center's elegant restaurant, Windows on the World. She was only 34. A senior associate at Jennison Associates, a financial services firm, she had been attending a technology conference at the World Trade Center when a plane struck Tower 1, shutting her up in a sepulcher in the sky. I lit a *yahrzeit* candle to commemorate the anniversary of her death. Jews believe that the soul of the departed derives joy from the kindling of lights. Her soul is God's candle.

At the end of the day, Rick shook me from my ruminations. He told me that Nash had called him from the U.S. Attorney's Office and

151

said the criminal case was closed and that they no longer had an active investigation.

I was just stunned. No explanation was offered as to why, why *now*, what they were ever going to charge me with in the first place, or what made them decide not to. I have my hunches, of course. There was a lot going on in the atmospherics. The *New York Times Magazine* was about to publish a sympathetic story on my situation, which the dropping of the investigation effectively killed because, in the words of the editor, "her life is no longer being held hostage." Bruce Fein had been shopping around to various media outlets the "Motion to Inspect and Copy" the secret leak report – which was being used to ruin me personally and professionally – to see if they wanted to sign on as petitioners. He was sure that the Justice Department had gotten wind of it by now. Ashcroft had just wrapped up his dog-and-pony show touting the Patriot Act (in August he set out on an unusual publicity blitz in which he stumped for the Act in 32 cities in more than 20 states, including election "swing" states) and President Bush had just endorsed the proposed "Patriot Act II." I was, and remain, on Congressional lists to testify against it.

Or perhaps it was because John Richter, the Chief of Staff for the Justice Department's Criminal Division (and later Acting Assistant Attorney General of the Criminal Division) came to a block party my family hosted and saw that I wasn't such a pariah after all. Our kids jumped together on the Moon Bounce in my front yard as his wife tended to their daughter in our kitchen. Anyway, I'll never know for sure why the case was dropped. What I *do* know for sure is that, still, no one has ever meaningfully investigated the underlying issue of the cover-up I exposed, ever.

"As quickly as it began, it ended," my husband said. I'd like to say we were both relieved, but neither of us had any trust in the government's word. The next step would be for Rick to send the prosecutor something in writing memorializing their conversation because we were never going to get a letter clearing me. I'd like to say we celebrated, but it's impossible to really celebrate anything on September 11th. We went to Bob's Famous Ice Cream and ate cotton candy sherbet in relative silence with our kids. It was a quiet acknowledgement, but the main thing I felt was loss.

Everyone thought my ordeal was over when the criminal investigation ended. All I had to do was to start picking up the pieces of my life – no small task, but at least I could move forward. How naïve I was to think that this vindictive Administration was through with me.

The dropping of the criminal case strengthened our motion because the government could no longer argue that unsealing the secret leak report would interfere with an ongoing investigation. There was no longer any conceivable reason to keep the report under seal. Mona also favored filing the motion because it could reveal the degree to which Hawkins acted as the alter ego of the government. At the end of September, Rick asked the Justice Department whether its Office

153

of Professional Responsibility was conducting an investigation into my whistleblower allegations, as the *New York Times* had reported back during the Chertoff proceedings.

I had been out of work for nearly a year, and was hopeful that I could get a job. But those hopes were dashed on October 1, 2003, when I was surprisingly rejected by the law firm that had courted me. Despite their bravado, it turns out that they were just as cowardly as the rest. They didn't even have the courage or the courtesy to call me. Instead, I received an e-mail: "You're obviously a very capable attorney. But accusations about you, however unfounded, could complicate [your representation of our client] . . . The very public nature . . . would lead to media scrutiny. . . The risks here are too great considering our client's stake in regaining his life." How disappointing that they caved. It confirmed what my lawyers had been trying gently to tell me: I had been blacklisted.

High Holy Days dawned again. The rabbi implored, "Keep my tongue from evil and my lips from deceit. Help me be silent in the face of derision," the rabbi said. I hoped that *I* could take those words to heart.

The Yom Kippur *Kol Nidre* service reminded me that "for transgressions of one human being against another, the Day of Atonement does not atone until they have made peace with one another." I was not holding my breath that anyone would seek my forgiveness or try to make amends with me. So I instead focused on the passage that dealt with my responsibility of forgiving all who had hurt me, all who had wronged me, whether deliberately or inadvertently, whether by word or by deed: Claudia Flynn, Joan Goldfrank, Ron Powell, Glenn Fine, Cullen MacDonald, Michael Chertoff. It was a long list and none of them, at least half of whom are Jewish, sought *my* forgiveness. Not that I expected them to. Apologizing is not the forte of this Administration.

The rabbi's sermon was on enemy combatants, xenophobia and the evils of the Patriot Act. I felt as if it had been custom-written for me. For once, I didn't feel like such a bête noire. I sent Rabbi Reiner my latest law review article on enemy combatants and told him about my situation. He immediately called me at home.

An October 9th memo on "Interrogation Rules of Engagement," which each military intelligence officer at Abu Ghraib was asked to sign, set out in detail the wide range of pressure tactics approved in September and available before the rules were changed on October 12th. While it states that "at no time will detainees be treated inhumanely nor maliciously humiliated," it permits the use of yelling, loud music, a reduction of heat in winter and air conditioning in summer, and "stress positions" for as long as 45 minutes every four hours – all without first obtaining the permission of anyone more senior than the interrogation officer in charge at Abu Ghraib. At Guantánamo, interrogators needed approval from a two-star general (at least in theory) before they could use tactics such as isolating prisoners, reversing their sleep patterns

Towards the end of October, when I flew to a family function in New Mexico, I was pulled aside during passenger screening for a more extensive search than the usual stroll through the metal detector. I didn't think twice about it. I remembered Israeli security forces arresting a young Palestinian who was planning to disguise herself as a pregnant woman, with a bomb hidden in her falsely enlarged belly. It made sense that my being seven months pregnant raised suspicions.

When I returned home, I got a letter from the Justice Department's Office of Professional Responsibility. It acknowledged the receipt of Rick's letter of September 29th, in which he inquired about whether they were conducting an investigation of my whistleblower allegations that Justice officials withheld documents from the court, and retaliated against me because of the advice I rendered regarding Lindh's interrogation and because I notified Department officials of my belief that they had failed to produce several e-mails to the court.

The blind-side came in the next paragraph: "Please be advised that we have referred Ms. Radack to the bar [disciplinary authorities] of the District of Columbia and Maryland, of which we understand she is a member."

They also wrote, laughably, that, "We take allegations of misconduct by Department personnel very seriously, and we are investigating Ms. Radack's allegations." They admitted that they had been aware of my allegations for nearly eight months, but only now "anticipate commencing interviews in the near future."

Apparently, that's how seriously the Department takes allegations of official misconduct: they respond by punishing the whistleblower.

Despite OPR's inexplicable delay in investigating my very serious allegations regarding destruction of evidence and obstruction of justice, their office somehow found time to refer me to the state bars to which I belong. The Justice Department blackballed me in the legal community. They were now going after my license to practice law. As Elaine Cassel of Civil Liberties Watch wrote about my situation:

> Ashcroft has struck back at people who went over his head to report misconduct of federal prosecution witnesses, one in a terrorist case, one not. Both professionals, both are facing sanctions from their professional bodies at this time. They absolutely did the right thing, in the name of principled justice. Ashcroft did not get the verdicts he wanted, in some measure because of the actions these professionals took. But he is getting back at them. Even if they are proven to have done no wrong (and experts I have spoken to believe that they are innocent of wrongdoing), the fact that they are under investigation

159

must be reported to malpractice carriers and, in some states, to clients.

The OPR letter explained: "The Department believes that Ms. Radack violated her duty not to knowingly reveal attorney-client privileged information (*i.e.*, confidential information of the United States) . . . by leaking internal Department e-mails regarding the Lindh interrogation to *Newsweek*."

The referral letters themselves were based on the secret leak investigation, which was still under seal with the Lindh court and to which I did not have access. I could identify with the Guantánamo detainees who were being held indefinitely on the basis of evidence they weren't allowed to see. It felt like a procedure from the 15th-century Star Chamber.

The Department "summarized" the report and shared details of what the IG "determined" and what "the government concluded." The referral letter then added a curious footnote that "the information regarding the leak investigation contained in this letter is not 6(e) [secret grand jury] material," as if that somehow excused the Department's disclosure of information that was still under court seal. The government committed the same offense – disclosing materials under court seal to a non-government entity – of which it was accusing me. Moreover, the government had yet again disclosed its investigation to third parties: Hawkins, the media, and now the state bars. It was so hypocritical, on top of being vindictive.

160

I was 30 weeks pregnant. I couldn't eat or sleep and lost five pounds during the next week – not a good thing when you're supposed to be gaining a pound a week. I had an emergency sonogram to make sure the baby was still growing.

Rick Robinson wrote back to OPR that we found their letter both inadequate and disturbing. He pointed out that, although the Office of Professional Responsibility "take[s] allegations of misconduct by Department personnel very seriously," it had been more than seven months since my allegations regarding the concealment by officials in PRAO of documents relating to the Lindh prosecution and subsequent retaliation against me were referred to OPR. Rick also pointed out how startling we found their admission that they had yet to conduct *any* interviews into my allegations; in fact, it was doubtful that they would have undertaken any further investigation but for the letter of inquiry Rick had sent.

It appeared, instead, that they had spent the last seven months investigating *me* -- the very type of retaliatory activity we had hoped they would expose rather than perpetuate. The fact that they referred me to the bar disciplinary authorities without even having requested any information from me indicated that their office had little interest in knowing all the facts and circumstances surrounding my allegations of misconduct at PRAO.

More fundamentally, we had already disproved several of the key facts underlying their bar referral, which is something of which

161

their office should have been aware given that, by its own admission, it was working hand-in-glove with the IG. For example, it was false to say that Department investigators did not interview me. Agent Powell interviewed me on June 27, 2002. Likewise, I explained the facts surrounding the phone calls and fax transmission between Hawkins and *Newsweek* to my Hawkins supervisors, who interviewed me at the direction of the IG and then shared the information I provided to them with the IG. The bar referral was based on purely circumstantial evidence, including the same "smoking fax" the Inspector General had earlier used to get me fired from Hawkins, which we already proved was nothing more than my law review article.

We copied the bars on a response we sent to the Office of Professional Responsibility and explained that the Justice Department had no legal or factual basis for suggesting that I violated the confidentiality rule, and that its referral of me was just a continuation of a series of retaliatory actions in violation of the Whistleblower Protection Act and other federal laws.

A defensive Office of Professional Responsibility (OPR) responded that they began their investigation of my allegations on March 7, 2003, and were prepared to commence interviews in May, but that they had to hold their investigation in abeyance because of the criminal investigation of *me*. This claim was a classic example of blaming the victim. If OPR had bothered to do even a cursory look into my allegations in a timely fashion, rather than waiting, the government would have concluded much earlier that it had no basis for criminally charging me and could have begun investigating those who were truly criminally culpable in this matter, and who remain unexamined to this day. The government would have also unearthed evidence that was exculpatory to the bar referrals.

OPR disagreed that we invalidated several of the key "facts" underlying their referral, but did not give specifics, and refused to withdraw their bar referrals.

Finally, they claimed that they did not violate the court's sealing order by providing the substance of the leak investigation to Bar Counsel, but instead insisted that they offered only "documentary evidence" that already "exists in Department files independent of the October 11, 2002 report" – a distinction without a difference. They even supplied court authority in support of their disclosure in spite of a sealing order. Back-peddling from and downplaying their violation of the court's sealing order was just that – a thinly-veiled attempt to cover up more misconduct.

After all this damage had been done, to add insult to injury, the Office of Professional Responsibility said that they were now, finally, ready to interview me as part of their investigation into my allegations.

Given that they would risk violating the court's sealing order so that they could provide false and defamatory information to the bar authorities, I couldn't realistically expect them to conduct an objective and thorough review of *my*

163

allegations of misconduct at PRAO and of retaliatory actions by components of the Department of Justice, which now, unfortunately, appeared to include their office. It showed extremely bad faith to shoot first and ask questions later. They referred me to the state bar authorities before investigating the conduct that formed the basis of those referrals. It is obvious that they had a vested interest in discrediting me in order to bolster their own accusations.

Of course, Michael Chertoff, Claudia Flynn and Joan Goldfrank were never similarly referred to their respective state bars for violation of multiple provisions of the Model Rules of Professional Conduct governing candor toward the tribunal; fairness to opposing party and counsel; special responsibilities of a prosecutor; responsibilities of managers and supervisory lawyers; and misconduct. Nor have they ever been meaningfully investigated for what happened in the Lindh case.

This pattern is common in the Bush regime. Everyone in President Bush's war clique is untouchable: Defense Secretary Donald Rumsfeld, Deputy Defense Secretary Paul Wolfowitz, Undersecretaries of Defense Douglas Feith and Stephen Cambone, and National Security Advisor Condoleeza Rice. "The Vulcans" – the name Bush's national security cabal came up with for themselves – is an allusion to the TV science fiction show *Star Trek*. A humanoid race, the Vulcans have developed a culture dedicated to the complete mastery of logic, learning to suppress their emotions in nearly every aspect of their existence. They are secretive and perpetual liars.

14. Broken Wings

On December 24, 2003, military lawyers prepared a letter to the International Committee of the Red Cross, responding to the Red Cross' concern about conditions at Abu Ghraib prison. The military letter, signed by Brigadier General Janis Karpinski, contended that isolating some inmates at the prison for interrogation because of their significant intelligence value was a "military necessity," and said prisoners held as security risks could legally be treated differently from prisoners of war or ordinary criminals. The result of this policy was that Abu Ghraib became a macrocosm of what happened to John Walker Lindh.

On December 28th, I gave birth to an amazing, beautiful, perfect baby girl. The doctors administered a high dose of corticosteroids to me to try to stave off an MS exacerbation, which I had experienced following the birth of each of my boys.

While I was still in the hospital, Bruce Fein filed the Motion to Inspect and Copy the government's secret leak report. The Motion asked the judge in the John Walker Lindh case to unseal the report detailing the government's investigation of my conduct, which had been used to thoroughly smear me, and to appoint a special prosecutor to investigate the

Department's contempt of court. In the Motion, I revealed myself as *Newsweek's* source – the truth will set you free – and explained in detail why I was entitled to do so under federal whistleblowing law. I also finally told my version of events – the condensed, impersonal, and sanitized "legalese" version of what I have written here. On New Year's Eve, we sent a copy of the Motion to the state bar authorities as part of my response. I thought it a fitting way to begin 2004.

In March, my 84-year-old grandfather died tragically in a fire, so I flew to Georgia for the funeral. On the way down, I was singled out for a full-body pat-down search and told that I had been "randomly selected." The screener asked me if I was wearing an underwire bra. I said yes. She said she would have to feel it for verification. I asked her to please not press too hard because I was breastfeeding and it would trigger my let-down reflex.

Meanwhile, my fashionable Medela "Pump In Style" was being sent back and forth through the x-ray machine.

"It's a breastpump," I explained. Attorney General Ashcroft, who ordered the Justice Department to cover the semi-nude statue of the lady Spirit of Justice, may have a problem with the female breast, but surely baggage screeners, many of them women, would be more enlightened.

When I later opened the luggage I had checked, the lock had been broken off and there was a note from the Transportation Security Administration (TSA) explaining that my suitcase had been hand-searched. A plastic blue "lock" had then been placed on the suitcase as a "courtesy." It seemed invasive, but tolerable because it was for security's sake.

During the return flight, I was again told that I'd been "randomly selected" for a more elaborate search. "Randomness" was becoming pretty predictable. Randomness, in the true sense of the word, has no specific pattern or objective. Randomness is a phenomenon that does not produce the same outcome or consequences every time it occurs under identical circumstances. Randomness is unsystematic.

Before my next flight less than a week later, I became aware that the airlines administered a "no-fly" list designed to keep terrorism suspects off commercial airlines, which subjected scores of innocent passengers to repeated interrogation, detention and stigmatization. The "no-fly" list is one of two maintained by the TSA, part of the Department of Homeland Security, which the Justice Department oversees. The other is the "selectee" list. Those on the "no-fly" list are not allowed to board commercial aircraft. Those on the "selectee" list must go through more extensive screening before boarding. Homeland Security officials will not confirm or deny that you are on the "no-fly" list, and will not discuss the criteria they use to put people on the list, except to say that it identifies people suspected of posing "a risk of air piracy or terrorism or a threat to airline or passenger safety."

When I went through security for my flight

to California a few days later, I was again pulled aside for a full-body wand search. With respect to my carry-on bag, they wanted to know why I had a breastpump but no milk and no baby. I explained that *that* was precisely the point: I couldn't bring my infant on the trip, so I was going to collect and store milk for her during my travels. On the way back, the screeners looked at my boarding pass and again singled me out for a more extensive search.

I specifically asked the screener if I was on the "no-fly" or "selectee" list. She didn't disabuse me of that notion; instead, she just told me she did not know. I had two full baby bottles of breastmilk in the refrigeration compartment of my breastpump. A male screener asked me if I would be willing to take a sip from each. This was months before a similar scene appeared in Michael Moore's movie, "Farenheit 9/11."

"Are you serious?" I asked.

I requested to see a copy of the written policy in which passengers are asked to personally sample liquids they take through security. I figured that if there were a policy governing suspect liquids, the screeners would be specially equipped with sterile droppers from which they could take a sample of my breastmilk to make sure it wasn't an organic peroxide, which is a low-power explosive with unusual stability problems. But these screeners were obviously not really concerned that my milk was, for example, perchloric acid, an odorless watery white liquid that can be dangerously reactive. If they harbored such a concern, they would not have asked me to open the bottle because it would have blown a hole in the building.

There was no scientific basis for the drink-your-own-breastmilk test. Passengers take through security everything from beverages to hand lotion to nasal spray. Knowing there was no lactation policy, I further objected because drinking from the sterile baby bottles would contaminate the milk, the milk was for the baby, I'm lactose intolerant, and it formed, overall, a barbaric request.

At that point, the screener's supervisor said he would check the milk in a different way, which he did by rubbing a white cloth all over the bottles and the breastpump. I can only surmise that the cloth was meant to pick up traces of chemicals or hazardous material, which of course it did not. I was finally allowed to board.

I'm on the "selectee" list. Of course, I have no way of verifying that for certain, or of getting my name removed. One might think that I'm being overly paranoid, but not when I explain that I am a former Department of Justice attorney and whistleblower in a high-profile terrorism case. The "selectee" list was just the latest example in which I have been designated as a suspect without any sort of due process. I share this dubious distinction with the likes of Anthony Romero, Executive Director of the ACLU, Senator Kennedy and various members of the Green Party. It is more than an inconvenience. It is political punishment.

Getting stopped twice in less than a week

for the extended dance version of the security search seems *not* like a way to stop passengers who pose a security risk, but more like a way to detain, interrogate, delay, embarrass, harass and humiliate perceived political enemies. That's what happens when the Bush Administration labels dissenters as unpatriotic. Politics becomes a proxy for suspicion. Our leaders fail to realize that it makes us all less safe to devote so much time and energy, and so limited resources, to vengeful partisan practices rather than going after people with *real* terrorist ties. The government's long campaign of investigation and harassment against me exemplifies the wasteful and anti-democratic nature of the Bush Administration's ill-defined war on terrorism.

On April 28, 2004, Deputy Solicitor General Paul Clement argued three so-called "enemy combatant cases" before the Supreme Court. Justice Ruth Bader Ginsburg asked him a prophetic question: "Suppose the executive says, 'Mild torture, we think, will help get this information,'" she queried. "Some systems do that to get information."

"Well, our executive doesn't" Clement replied. "And I think the fact that executive discretion in a war situation can be abused is not a good and sufficient reason for judicial micromanagement in overseeing of the authority. You have to recognize that in situations where there is a war, where the government is on a war footing, that you have to trust the executive." Even though top military officials knew of the Abu Ghraib prisoner abuse at least as early as January 2004, defense officials deliberately hid knowledge of it from Clement, making him unwittingly mislead the Court.

In an example of perfect irony, that evening, *60 Minutes II* aired the explosive photographs of detainees in the American-run Abu Ghraib prison outside of Baghdad, Iraq. The release of these photographs dovetailed with the May 10, 2004 issue of *The New Yorker*, in which Pulitzer Prize-winning journalist Seymour Hersh blew the Abu Ghraib prison abuse scandal wide open. These two events sent shock waves around the world.

15. The Tide Slowly Turns

A number of pivotal events influenced my situation and validated the advice I originally rendered in the Lindh case. None of these events standing alone ended my story, but taken together, they all worked to turn the tide of public opinion and prodded people to at least cast a jaundiced eye upon the conduct of the Administration in the war on terrorism. The judicial branch stopped acting as a rubber stamp of whatever the executive branch did and at long last, Congress awoke from its deep slumber.

In addition to the explosive *60 Minutes II* and Seymour Hersh's article, the torture memos started leaking out in a steady drumbeat of horror.

"*Finally*," I thought with a sigh of relief. I cried tears of joy that I was no longer alone, howling into the darkness with my complaint that the United States was taking shortcuts of the worst kind. But I also cried tears of despair that it was so much more widespread than what happened to John Walker Lindh.

On June 1, 2004, James Comey, Deputy Attorney General for the Department of Justice, held a news conference concerning U.S. citizen Jose Padilla, a former Chicago gang member held by the U.S. as an "enemy combatant" for two years. Comey had been the U.S. Attorney back when Padilla was first arrested on a material witness warrant. Comey's press conference was ostensibly in response to a letter from Senator Hatch requesting information about American citizens being held on U.S. soil as enemy combatants. But public skepticism about the suspicious timing of the press conference suggests that it was a backdoor way to influence the Supreme Court, which was close to ruling on Padilla's case, and to deflect attention from a melodramatic press conference given by Ashcroft and Mueller a week earlier, which was criticized by many for overstating the al Qaeda threat in order to influence the upcoming presidential election.

As I listened to the news conference, I couldn't believe my ears. Comey's words echoed exactly the concerns I originally voiced in the Lindh case.

"Why don't you bring criminal charges against him now?" a reporter asked.

"I'm not ruling out that criminal charges might be an option some day," Comey responded. "We, obviously, can't use any of the statements he's made in military custody . . ."

Oh really? Such a conclusion was not so obvious, or apparent at all, to Ashcroft and Chertoff in the Lindh case.

When later asked if the government had plans to present the information from Comey's press conference to a grand jury, Comey reiterated the problem with this course of action: "I don't believe that we could use this information in a criminal case, because we

174

deprived him of access to his counsel and questioned him in the absence of counsel. . . This was done not to make . . . a criminal case against Jose Padilla. It was done to find out the truth about what he knew about al Qaeda and threats to the United States."

"How does your refusal to grant access to an attorney for him throughout the process fit into this?" another reporter asked. "You have now indicated that he may have access, as I understand it, and . . ."

"And he's had access to counsel," Comey said.

"[T]hat being the case, if you're not going to bring charges any time soon, for reasons that you've explained, and yet he has access to counsel, where does that leave him in the long run?" the reporter asked.

"I'm not [foreclosing] bringing a criminal case," Comey explained. "What I was saying was, I don't believe we can use his statements made in military custody against him. So if there's a criminal case to be made separate and apart from that, perhaps that's an option."

Comey's statements about access to counsel and not mixing military intelligence-gathering with civilian prosecution in a criminal court reflected exactly the concerns I expressed in the Lindh matter, and a complete reversal from what Ashcroft and Chertoff said and did two years earlier in the Lindh case.

A few weeks later, the government was caught off guard when the Supreme Court ruled in the trio of "enemy combatant" cases on June 28, 2004. While the Court affirmed the President's authority to detain enemy combatants in the war on terrorism, it ruled that the latter have the right to challenge their detention in U.S. court and that they have the right to counsel. The ruling was a major blow for Bush.

In a six-to-three decision against the Administration, the Supreme Court ruled that the more-than-600 detainees from over 42 different countries held at the United States naval base at Guantánamo Bay could appeal to federal courts, with the assistance of a lawyer, that they were being held unlawfully.

In Padilla's case, the Court sidestepped the merits of his case on a jurisdictional technicality.

But in the matter of Yaser Hamdi, who was captured along with John Walker Lindh on the same day at the same place in Afghanistan, his case resulted in a landmark Supreme Court defeat for the White House. The Court ruled eight-to-one that Hamdi should have an opportunity to rebut before a neutral party the government's case for detaining him. Four court members would have even released him, arguing that his detention was unlawful. Justice Sandra Day O'Connor wrote for the majority, "We have long since made clear that a state of war is not a blank check for the President when it comes to the rights of the nation's citizens." Significantly, she stated that Hamdi "unquestionably has the right to access to counsel," a question that had been at the heart of my advice in the Lindh case.

Less than four months after telling the Supreme Court that holding Yaser Hamdi in military custody was crucial to national security and the war on terrorism, the government released him back to Saudi Arabia. The decision to set Hamdi free stood in stark contrast to the two decades Lindh was serving in prison. Buoyed by Hamdi's release, lawyers for Lindh filed a request for clemency with the Bush administration, asking that his 20-year sentence (the second-longest term handed down in the war on terrorism) be commuted.

16.   Victories

On July 14, 2004, I reached a settlement with Hawkins, Delafield and Wood. The sticking point all along had been their insistence that I forego my ability to write about my experience. I said that the truth was worth more to me than their money. The settlement preserved my right to speak. I used the entire proceeds of the settlement to pay off my attorney's fees owed to Fulbright & Jaworski.

The threat of terrorism continued to touch my family in a very personal way. On August 1, 2004, the government raised the terror alert level for the World Bank, where Dan worked, and four other financial institutions, citing the discovery of remarkably detailed intelligence showing that al Qaeda operatives had been plotting for years to blow up specific buildings with car or truck bombs. It was hard to lie to the kids about why Daddy's easily-recognizable office building was on TV every night.

The Justice Department asked a judge on August 31, 2004, to throw out the convictions of a suspected terrorist "sleeper cell" in Detroit because of prosecutorial misconduct, reversing course in a case the Bush administration once hailed as a major victory in the war on terrorism. The department's decision came after a months-long independent investigation uncovered potentially exculpatory discoverable evidence that prosecutors withheld from defense lawyers before the trial, and exposed deep differences within the government over the course of the case and the quality of the prosecution's evidence. It sounded all too familiar. Another celebrated prosecution in the war on terrorism imploded.

With the Hawkins thread of my yarn out of the way and with my legal bills paid off, Fulbright & Jaworski generously agreed to represent me *pro bono* in suing the Department of Justice. It was incredibly empowering to read the complaint: *Radack v. Department of Justice.* I filed the suit on October 28, 2004, a date that we pointed out to the Maryland and D.C. bar associations marked the fact that they had now sat on the complaints against me for more than a year. It turned out, in fact, that Maryland had put the complaint on its "deferred docket."

Whether prompted by my lawsuit, or Bush's re-election, both the Maryland and D.C. Bars were soon ready to hear from me. Their decisions drove up my anxiety level more than the criminal investigation, which was scary but always abstract. My weight dropped below 100 pounds, I had to take sleeping pills at night, and even then I regularly had nightmares about the bar proceedings. I cried a lot during the days, yelled at the kids, and wrecked the car. Three years and $100,000 worth of law school, nearly a decade of professional training and work, and my very ability to practice law were at stake.

The irony of the bar proceedings is that I learned a lot of damning information that the Justice Department had studiously avoided providing to me, and that ultimately cleared me.

179

Through the operation of the bar machinery, we finally obtained a copy of the coveted OIG Report, which the Justice Department had used to tarnish me to my law firm and to the bar associations. We had only procured a "summary" of it previously with Bruce Fein's motion. The full version was so ludicrous, sloppy and riddled with holes and contradictions that it actually made the bar complaints easy to defend. We detailed the numerous inaccuracies, exaggerations and inconsistencies in a lengthy response we prepared for the bars.

But the OIG Report provided more than just potent ammunition to use in the bar proceedings. It provided the biggest missing pieces of the puzzle. Just as Chertoff's judicial confirmation hearing answered the question of how high up the chain of command the malfeasance went in my case, and just as the torture memos filled in the backdrop of my story, the OIG Report answered the question of motive, about which I could only speculate before.

First, it contained an e-mail that I had never seen in which De Pue told Patty Merkamp Stemler, Chief of the Criminal Division's Appellate Section, "[W]e have committed an ethical violation."

Second, and most importantly, it contained the sworn affidavit of John De Pue, someone I had often wondered about, but never dared to contact throughout this mess. Was he suffering any of the same fallout that I was over my advice? Did our exchange alter his life, personally or professionally?

180

In his sworn statement, De Pue says: "[In] January 2002, Jim Reynolds [Chief of the Terrorism & Violent Crime Section] informed me that the Criminal Division's leadership was disturbed that I had sought PRAO's advice in this matter."

I always knew that my superiors had the means and opportunity to get rid of the damning e-mail, but I could only hypothesize that their motive was to bury evidence that conflicted with the party line the Justice Department ultimately decided to take. Now I had their motive in black and white. Here was a sworn statement that the "Criminal Division's leadership" was upset about the advice I gave.

I mailed the juicy tidbits from the report to Eric Lichtblau of the *New York Times*. I knew it wasn't enough for him to write a story, but I wanted to let him know that he was right in believing me back during Chertoff's confirmation and that Chertoff was lying and covering-up. I thought it would perhaps be helpful background for future war on terrorism articles. I never expected an actual story to come of it.

17.   Chertoff Redux

What had been personal validation for me became very public fodder when President Bush selected Michael Chertoff on January 11, 2005, to head the Office of Homeland Security. My e-mail "In" box lit up like a switchboard. That was a Tuesday. My Maryland bar hearing was three days later.

The next day, newspapers, Internet websites, and TV and radio programs were calling, asking for my thoughts on Chertoff.

This time I spoke up.

Eric Lichtblau called and said he was writing something for the *New York Times*. For me, that was the gold standard. It didn't matter if no one else covered it. It gave me the courage and fortitude to speak out. I did a radio show that evening, tentatively describing what happened the last time Chertoff was nominated.

On Thursday morning, Eric's article appeared in the *New York Times*. It was amazing. Not only did he document Chertoff's lies to Congress the last time around, but also he got John De Pue to speak on the record about what happened. It was the first time De Pue had commented publicly.

"The front office was unhappy with the fact that I had gone to PRAO with my inquiry," De Pue said. "I was more or less told that I was out of line in making that inquiry. It was not a popular thing to do, but I thought at the time it was the reasonable thing to do. We'd been told time after time that if an ethics issue arose, the people in that office were the ones to see."

The supervisor who conveyed the displeasure of the Criminal Division's leadership "did not use Chertoff's name," De Pue explained, "but I certainly inferred from what he said that the unhappiness was coming from Chertoff."

The next four paragraphs all but called Chertoff a liar:

> At his confirmation hearing for the appellate judgeship, Mr. Chertoff said he was not aware of the dissent among department lawyers on the case, including an opinion from an ethics lawyer, Jesselyn Radack, saying an F.B.I. interview of Mr. Lindh would not be authorized under the law.

> Mr. Chertoff said, "I was not consulted with respect to this matter," and he said he was unaware that the office that handled ethics issues had given an official opinion on interviewing Mr. Lindh without his lawyer.

> "I do not recall anyone expressing the opinion that the F.B.I. should be stopped from interviewing John Walker Lindh because of professional ethics rules

183

about contacts with represented persons," he said in a written response to Senator Edward M. Kennedy, Democrat of Massachusetts. Mr. Chertoff defended the propriety of the interview, saying at his hearing it was highly unlikely "that a lawyer was going to be flown into the battlefield in Afghanistan."

Senator Kennedy briefly held up Mr. Chertoff's nomination in part because of the questioning, saying he found some answers about the case "nonresponsive, evasive and hypertechnical."

I even got the last word, literally, in the article: "It's incredible to me that we would want someone leading the Department of Homeland Security who gives equivocal and misleading statements to Congress and avoids answering the tough questions." It was a good soundbyte compared to what I really wanted to say, which was, "If confirmed as Secretary of Homeland Security, I hope that Chertoff takes my name off the 'no-fly' list."

The article painted Chertoff as who he really is and would hopefully provoke questioning at his confirmation hearing. Just as important, the article could not have been better timed with the Maryland Bar's "Peer Review Panel" meeting the next day.

I felt like my grandfather was watching out for me from above. I went on two radio programs that day, "Democracy Now" and "Air America." I declined to go on an MSNBC show that night. The "Peer Review Panel" meeting was the next morning.

I drove to Baltimore with Rick for the meeting. We passed Eric's article out to the panel first thing. Even though it wasn't a formal hearing, the members treated the panel like a trial, with opening and closing statements by Rick and the Assistant Bar Counsel, who was standing in for the usual attorney, Gail, who had been investigating my case for over a year. The panel asked a lot of good questions about why I didn't go directly to the Court, what my state of mind was when I made my disclosure, and why I chose *Newsweek* as the medium to blow the whistle.

I was as cool as a cucumber. At one point, the Assistant Bar Counsel, who was acting as the prosecutor, said, "No misconduct by Justice has ever been proven."

"Journalists have proved it," I fired back. "Congress has proved it. Who else has to prove it? That burden can't be on me." My voice was forceful and calm.

Someone else on the panel suggested that mine would be a good test case for confidentiality obligations with regard to whistleblowing. I politely explained that I'd already spent $50,000 litigating this over the past three years, and that I did not think that this proceeding should be continued at my expense just because it presented a novel issue.

185

During the panel's deliberations, the Assistant Bar Counsel said they were thinking along the lines of reprimanding me, to which we promptly said we would not agree. He said the best we could hope for was a "conditional diversion agreement," whereby I would agree to some sort of punishment. He could not think of what exactly that punishment would look like: Not practice law for a while? I had been sidelined for the past three years. Teach about Rule 1.6 on confidentiality? I had already been doing that. And would they want someone teaching about a rule she had supposedly violated?

But even if we could fashion some viable diversionary agreement conditioned on my doing (or refraining from doing) something, I would still have to admit wrongdoing.

"For what?" I asked over and over again. "I want to know what it is, exactly, that I did wrong."

I said that I would be amenable to a dismissal with some sort of warning (to be more careful, to seek an informal bar opinion before I took a controversial action, *etc.*) A half hour later, Rick and I were ready to leave and were surprised to find that the panel had just adjourned. They had told us they would need six or seven hours to deliberate, but they took only 30 minutes. On our way out, one member shook my hand and said what an honor it was to meet me. Another member said he didn't expect to find that someone so "diminutive" had done "all this." The non-attorney member of the panel whispered to Rick that they found the charges "without merit."

Towards the end of the day, Rick called the Assistant Bar Counsel, who said that his boss would think about a conditional diversion agreement, or because Maryland just adopted a choice-of-law provision under which D.C. rules would govern my conduct, they might fob the case off on D.C.

I was livid. If Maryland was going to kick the case to D.C., I'd rather it be because it was "without merit," than on jurisdictional grounds. Rick said it was a good day for us nonetheless. But by now, I'd learned my lesson not to feel relieved prematurely – as I did when Lindh pleaded guilty (not because of the plea itself, but because it would end the government's abuse), when the OIG investigation concluded, when the criminal investigation was closed, and at numerous other junctures throughout this sordid tale.

I woke up every morning feeling panicky about the looming bar decision, my chest tight, my breathing rapid and my heart pounding. I went on an anxiety-induced cleaning binge to alleviate my nervousness waiting to hear from Rick. The house never looked so tidy.

A few days later, Rick told me that Gail took the case back from the Assistant Bar Counsel who had substituted for her. She wanted to reprimand me because I'm "not really a whistleblower." That infuriated me. She was not at the Peer Review Panel meeting, did not have the benefit of the three-hour hearing, and was buying off on the Justice Department's assertion that I was not a whistleblower – as if it was up to the accused entity to determine whether the whistleblower counted – an absurd notion. The bar complaint had gone from being "without merit," to being "without jurisdiction" – both of which would have resulted in dismissal – to reprimanding me.

Michael Powell from the New York bureau of the *Washington Post* then called me. Despite my situation being such an inside-the-Beltway story, the *Washington Post* had not touched it.

January 20, 2005 was Bush's second inauguration, so we did the only logical thing: skip town. On Monday, Rick and Gail called the Chair of the Peer Review Panel to tell him that there was no settlement and that the panel should go ahead and issue its report. The Chairman said that they actually had already been circulating a draft among themselves, which he thought would be final soon.

Rick asked if the Chair could tell him how it came out.

The Chair said he did not want to do so until all the members had approved the language of their report, but he added, "We did not hang anyone."

I continued to hold my breath, keep my fingers crossed, and write in my journal late, late into the night. I wrote 50 thank you notes for holiday gifts, read three novels, wrote a book review, emptied one hundred messages from my e-mailbox, labeled two thick photo albums worth of pictures, and continued to furiously clean the house. The waiting was unbearable. I was absolutely obsessing about the bar outcome.

Dreaming about it. Worrying about it. Dreading it. Needing it. It could be that week, but it could also be a long wait.

I received an ACLU online newsletter that said, "ACLU Leads Efforts to Stop Government Silencing of Whistleblowers." Like the *Washington Post*, the ACLU was one of those organizations that had been missing in action during most of my ordeal. I had even applied to them for a job and was told that I "really needed to put all this behind" me first. Again, I felt left out of the ACLU, left out of the "whistleblower community," left out, period, twisting in the wind.

On January 29, 2005, I received a copy of the Recommendation of the Peer Review Panel in connection with the complaint made against me in Maryland. The panel recommended that the matter be dismissed because, as to the charges involving Rule 8.4 (misconduct), there did not appear to be a substantial basis by which to conclude that I engaged in wrongdoing. As to the charges involving Rule 1.6 (confidentiality), the Peer Review Panel "found that there were indications that a breach of Rule 1.6 had occurred," but believed that it should be considered and adjudicated by the D.C. Bar for jurisdictional reasons. So, it was a mixed bag, but more of the better than the worse. It was now up to the Attorney Grievance Commission of Maryland to approve or disapprove the Peer Review Panel's recommendation.

On the morning of Chertoff's confirmation hearing, Powell's article ran in the *Washington Post*, with the headline *Chertoff Apt to Face*

Questions on Ethics. The subhead read: *Stance on Lindh Interrogation at Issue.*

Better late than never, I thought.

I couldn't stomach watching the hearing. But when a friend told me that my situation came up during the proceedings, I went to C-SPAN's website, held my nose, and listened to the entire three hours of testimony.

"Judge Chertoff," said Senator Akaka from Hawaii, "today's *Washington Post* reported on your role in the alleged retaliation against an employee of the Justice Department Professional Responsibility Advisory Office who disagreed with the DOJ interrogation policies. As the author of legislation to strengthen protections for federal whistleblowers, this troubles me."

Thank God, I thought.

"My question to you is, will you pledge to protect whistleblowers and foster an open work environment that promotes the disclosure of government mismanagement and government illegality?"

The questions were classic softballs. Akaka didn't ask whether the article was accurate, why I was being retaliated against, or who was responsible for the campaign of harassment.

But Chertoff swung at them with great force. He just couldn't help himself. "Senator, first, I had no part in any way, shape or form in any retaliation against this individual for any reason, let alone giving advice. I am pledged to support whistleblowers and to support candid assessments by employees when there are problems in the Department. In fact, I'd like to

190

hear about them first, because as I've said previously, we all make mistakes, and the only way we learn is if we get feedback, and I'd rather get the feedback to correct it than have people just simmer about it."

Chertoff was a soft-spoken and elegant liar. I was mad that he claimed to want "feedback" to correct "mistakes," which is exactly what I had provided. But the testimony that really infuriated me was when, upon being questioned about the Justice Department's infamous torture memo, he told Senator Levin, "You are dealing in an area where there's potential criminal liability. You had better be very careful to make sure that whatever it is you decide to do falls well within what is required by the law."

I couldn't believe my ears. What he was saying was unbelievable. But a minute later he reiterated, "You had better be sure that you have good faith and you've operated diligently to make sure what you are considering doing is well within the law."

Senator Levin continued his line of questioning and Chertoff continued to gild the proverbial lily. "[I]f you are dealing with something that makes you nervous, you'd better make sure that you are doing the right thing. And you'd better check it out, and that means doing an honest and diligent examination of what you're doing, and not really putting your head in the sand or turning a blind eye."

Chertoff is a hypocrite plain and simple. He was not a "true believer" like Ashcroft, whose actions never contradict their beliefs, or a

191

tautological rationalizer like Gonzales, who conform their beliefs around their actions to eliminate contradiction. He is a person who pretends publicly to have certain virtues and moral beliefs that he does not actually possess, and whose actions belie his stated principles.

I channeled my anger into a searing Op-Ed that ran in the *L.A. Times*. I did what I'd been so scared of doing for so long. I wrote a first-person account, and I lambasted Chertoff. It was a solid placement in a reputable newspaper. I knew it wouldn't make a difference in Chertoff's confirmation; after all, I'm a political realist. Despite being the unprovoked force behind the roundup of hundreds of Arab, South Asian and Muslim men after September 11th, and despite acknowledging that he was consulted on the development and implementation of the notorious torture memo, Chertoff was clearly the lesser of two evils compared to Alberto Gonzales, who had recently been confirmed as Attorney General. But at least I said my piece, and there's something incredibly empowering about that. It was only 18 paragraphs, but it was the most important thing I ever wrote. I was not going to sit in the corner and suck my thumb while Chertoff lied his way into yet another promotion.

Years later, I again heard Chertoff, in his capacity as Homeland Security Secretary, saying that he was unaware for several days of the severity of the flooding caused by Hurricane Katrina. There was a catastrophic delay of federal emergency measures, rescue efforts and aid to tens of thousands stranded New Orleans residents. If he lies about the "little" things, like my situation, of course he is going to lie about the big things. Why would anyone be surprised? The Category 3 storm killed 1,321 people, including 1,072 in Louisiana; displaced about 2 million people; and caused more than $150 billion in damage. Later Michael D. Brown, the embattled former director of the Federal Emergency Management Agency, which was absorbed by Chertoff's fiefdom, blew the whistle on Chertoff and other Bush officials for setting the country on a "path to failure" by over-emphasizing the threat of terrorism. Brown had been a Bush political loyalist who became the face of the government's failed Katrina response. He made his criticisms public. He named names.

The response to my Op-Ed was tremendous. It was reprinted on the Internet by a number of different websites and I received hundreds of supportive e-mails.

On February 15, 2005, Chertoff was confirmed 98-0. The next day, the Attorney Grievance Commission of Maryland dismissed the bar complaint against me. *This* time, I celebrated with confidence. The day after that, John De Pue, with whom I had exchanged the infamous e-mails, and *Newsweek* journalist Michael Isikoff, to whom I had leaked them, met each other at a New America Foundation event on "The Torture Papers." Their presence there spoke for itself and the life-transforming nature of the John Walker Lindh case.

18. Epilogue

People always ask me, "Knowing what you know now, would you still blow the whistle?"

My answer is yes. In a utilitarian sense, I realize this is completely irrational. It has wreaked havoc on my family, my health, my finances and my career. But in a deontological sense, it is right. As Robert Frost expressed in his poem *The Road Not Taken*, "Two roads diverged in a wood, and I – I took the one less traveled by, And that has made all the difference."

In discussing whistleblowing, it saddens and scares me when people I love, trust and respect say, "I don't know if I could do it."

My response is, without meaning to sound self-righteous, "How could you not?"

Small whistles can make big noises. I was willing to take a career risk out of a deeper loyalty to the American people. I was committed to the government's mission to serve the public and do "justice." I was simply doing my job and got caught sideways in Executive Branch politics. My true employer is the American taxpayer, not a bunch of political ideologues.

We learn from our leaders how not to accept responsibility. It is frightening to think that most people would stand by idly in the face of wrongdoing, rather than speak out. That is how we get days like 9/11 in the first place – by stifling meaningful dialogue and blinding ourselves to opposition. I am a canary in a coalmine. The expression derives from the old practice of using canaries to detect toxic or explosive gases in coalmines. More sensitive to such fumes than humans, canaries would collapse long before the miners were affected, and a fallen canary was a signal to miners to get out immediately, and to management to examine the problem and clean up the mine. I like to think of myself not as the poisoned canary, but rather as a luminous yellow bird that won't stop singing in the silent, dark and dirty bowels of this Administration and the troglodytes who occupy it. Although I often feel like I'm chirping into the darkness, at least I still have my voice. And I'm going to use it.

Author's Note

George W. Bush was re-elected as President of the United States.

Alberto Gonzales was confirmed 60-36 as Attorney General, making him the man with the second most "no" votes ever lodged against him as a successful nominee for Attorney General. (John Ashcroft had the dubious distinction of getting the most "no" votes when he was confirmed 58-42 in 2001).

Donald Rumsfeld is the only senior cabinet member to retain his post, Secretary of Defense, during Bush's second term.

Condoleeza Rice was promoted to Secretary of State.

Paul Wolfowitz, Deputy Defense Secretary, was made President of the World Bank.

Michael Chertoff, after leaving his seat as a federal appellate judge, was confirmed 98-0 as the new Secretary of Homeland Security.

Alice Fisher, Chertoff's protégé who worked alongside him in the mid-1990s as a staff lawyer on the Senate Whitewater investigation and who served as his deputy from 2001 until 2003, is the Assistant Attorney General for the Criminal Division, despite having no prosecutorial experience.   President Bush used a "recess appointment" to bypass her blocked nomination.

Jay S. Bybee, the Assistant Attorney General for the Office of Legal Counsel from 2001-2003, was rewarded with a lifetime appointment as a federal appellate judge in California.

William J. Haynes, II, the Department of Defense General Counsel who was directly involved in setting interrogation policies and oversaw the Pentagon working group that relied heavily on the reasoning in the torture memo, has also been nominated for a federal appeals court judgeship on the Fourth Circuit Court of Appeals.

John Yoo, after serving from 2001-2003 as Deputy Assistant Attorney General for the Justice Department's Office of Legal Counsel (Bybee's deputy), is now a professor at Berkeley's Boalt Hall Law School.

Lieutenant General Ricardo Sanchez, who was commander of American forces in Iraq at the time of the Abu Ghraib scandal, is being considered for promotion to the Southern Command, which comes with a fourth star.

Claudia Flynn received the 2005 Mary C. Lawton Lifetime Service Award and retired as the Director of the Justice Department's Professional Responsibility Advisory Office.

Joan Goldfrank became a Magistrate Judge on

the D.C. Family Court.

Betsy Plevan, Hawkins' attorney, became President of the nation's premier bar association, the very liberal Association of the Bar of the City of New York, which is working on the forefront of rights for "enemy combatants."

John De Pue remains at the Department of Justice.

Jesselyn Radack was elected to the D.C. Bar's Legal Ethics Committee in June 2005. She has twice provided testimony to Congress about her ordeal. She now works at Grayson & Kubli, representing whistleblowers in False Claims Act cases dealing with reconstruction fraud in Iraq.

John Walker Lindh remains in jail, serving out a 20-year sentence. In December 2005, he petitioned for commutation of his sentence.